I WAS A STRIPPER LIBRARIAN

From Cardigans to G-Strings

by Kristy Cooper

Published by Olivier.

ISBN: 978-0-578-94489-0

Personal names and some library names have been changed to protect the identities of the people I knew during this time in my life.

All strip club names, however, remain the same.

To all the other sex workers who have come out before me and have told their stories. And to all the sex workers who want to come out and tell their stories too.

"

I have always imagined that Paradise
will be a kind of library.

— Jorge Luis Borges

"

A truly great library contains something
in it to offend everyone.

— Jo Goodwin

~~~~~V~~~~~

Introduction

I first sat down to write down my recollections of my stripping career about seven years ago, which was seven years after I stripped. Although I completed the first draft of my manuscript at that time, I didn't show it to anyone. Instead, I set up a fake email with the name Penelope Pomegranate and began emailing agents with my query letter. I only ended up emailing about fifteen of them, and although I got a bite from one who had gotten successful memoirs published before, this endeavor ultimately led nowhere. It was just as well, though, because I had yet to form a plan on how I would actually deal with my real identity if this book were to be published.

At the time, an article I wrote was published in xoJane about my experiences and possible forthcoming book. I wouldn't let them pay me, though. I was afraid giving my real name and information in order to get paid would somehow come back to bite me in the butt, and I could be outed. I had this compulsion to tell my story and get it out there, but I wanted to somehow do that and not be officially associated with it. I clearly wasn't ready.

A big part of my impetus for writing this book is to destigmatize sex work and show that sex workers come from all walks of life. You probably already know someone who has done it, even if they're not out about it. But how could I destigmatize it for others when I wasn't ready to face the stigma myself?

Stigma and shame about having worked as a stripper kept me quiet for a long time. They also led me to isolating myself a lot more than I should have. I was afraid that if I got too close to people, they would find out what I did, and I would have to deal with their judgments. I was also afraid of how it would affect me professionally. As it was, I'd already had to jump through hoops to get a full-time library job, and obtaining full-time library work was becoming all the more precarious.

It's funny how shame works. I was never actually ashamed of stripping, but I was ashamed of how others might perceive me if they knew. It did not violate my personal morals, and I never felt like I had done anything wrong by doing this kind of job, but I was well aware that there were plenty of people who didn't approve, and I had the luxury of hiding it from them. I also didn't give people the chance to not approve, though, and didn't try to see if they would be understanding. The circles I ran in post-stripping did not include any former sex workers. This just wasn't something people talked about, so I assumed people wouldn't be open to it. However, I've learned that people who meet sex workers who are out are a lot more likely to be open-minded about sex work in general. I was trying to advocate while still remaining in the closet.

Since this initial attempt to tell my story, though, I've learned a lot more about my own power. I've gotten involved with several political-organizing and library-advocacy efforts that have helped me see just what kinds of changes I can make in the world. I learned that there is power in vulnerability and that I can definitely handle it if someone thinks I'm a big-jerk troublemaker because there are now plenty of people in this world who think exactly that about me, and I think it's funny more than anything else at this point.

Even within the last ten years, attitudes have changed. The library world is heavily focused on improving diversity, equity, and inclusion right now, which means a lot more librarians are open to listening to more marginalized experiences and perhaps not snapping to judgments on something they have no personal experience with. I was terrified to announce that this book was coming out to the library world, but I knew this was the first step I needed to take to ensure I finally finished and published this. I needed the social pressure of people knowing the book existed to finally put it out in the world.

I shared the book in the largest group for library workers on Facebook, and the response was overwhelmingly supportive. Over eight hundred people made positive reactions to it, and the comments were all encouraging. I also worried about reactions from my coworkers, but they were all positive too. If there were people who didn't like what I was doing, which I'm sure there were, they kept their thoughts to themselves.

Another cool thing that happened when I announced that this book was coming out was getting messages from other library workers thanking me for doing this because they were also former sex workers. I knew I wasn't the only one, but it was validating to know I wasn't alone and that telling this kind of story was going to help people in the library world, as well, and hopefully help more people from so-called respectable professions come out as former sex workers.

I want to recognize too that I'm a more privileged sex worker. I'm an educated white cis person from a middle-class background, with access to more social capital than those who have done subsistence sex work. Sex workers with backgrounds similar to mine predominate the stories that curious civilians read about sex work. We are more likely to find our way to a platform to share our experiences in our industries, so it's important that we do what we can to destigmatize sex work for all sex workers.

Why do I think destigmatizing is so important? Destigmatizing sex work makes the work safer for current sex workers, especially the most marginalized among us. Black trans sex workers face the greatest violence. They can be targeted for who they are, and do not have anyone to call for help because their job is illegal. The Combahee River Collective Statement (put together by a group of Black feminists in

1977) says "If Black women were free, it would mean that everyone else would have to be free since our freedom would necessitate the destruction of all the systems of oppression." At that time feminists were just beginning to analyze the intersections of multiple systems of oppressions but had not yet included trans people and sex workers in their analysis. Today, liberation organizers have evolved their work and more readily focus on the liberation of the most marginalized among us, to bring about the liberation of all. Although I hope this book can help normalize discussing sex work, I know that my experiences are still limited, and I want to encourage everyone who is interested in lifting up the voices of sex workers and marginalized sex workers to take a look at the Additional Resources section at the end of this book for further reading and social media accounts I would recommend following.

One critical step in destigmatizing sex work is to not make sex workers dehumanizing punch lines in jokes. It's so normal to joke about violence done to sex workers, especially ones that work on the street. The other day, I was watching a sitcom I like called Superstore. The show often tackles social justice issues adeptly while still being accessible and pretty damn funny. But during a particular episode, the store's manager, Glen, made a comment about how their store is better than another store because of all the dead hookers that show up in that store's dumpster. Would it be okay to make this kind of joke with any other population? Sex workers are seen as expendable, and that's what the problem is.

Another critical part of destigmatizing is changing mainstream feminism. Within feminism, there are those who we can identify as SWERFs: sex worker exclusionary radical feminists. This is someone who claims to be a feminist but who does not believe that women engaged in any form of voluntary sex work should be included in the fight for equality. This form of feminism is closely tied to the term TERF, which stands for trans-exclusionary radical feminism.

SWERFs and TERFs tend to go hand-in-hand their ideology is rooted in white carceral feminism.

Carceral feminists support the criminalization of sex work, which again affects the most marginalized among us, especially those working on the street. However, all sex workers are subject to harassment, assault, and arrest by police. Even strip clubs, which are supposed to be legal, are subject to vice raids, wherein the police can come in and arrest workers for public lewdness and then put their mugshots in the local online paper for their families and neighbors to see. It is time for us culturally to move past the white carceral feminism of the past and embrace true intersectional feminism.

The best way to support sex workers is to support decriminalization. Full decriminalization of sex work means repealing all criminal statutes regarding selling sex, buying sex, loitering to sell or solicit sex, and brothel keeping. It's important to note that decriminalization is different from legalization. Legalization sounds good, but it actually leads to regulations that still allow certain activities to be criminalized and require licenses that not everyone can easily obtain. Moreover, regulation still allows for sex workers to be surveilled by the state and subject to policing. This approach fundamentally misunderstands the historic violent role of law enforcement in the lives of sex workers. Most sex workers do not trust cops to help them in a crisis, plus there is the frequency with which law enforcement is likely to be the perpetrator of harm toward sex workers in the first place. I've frequently seen the statistic that 40 percent of police families experience domestic violence, but I don't know if people also know there is a study that also shows 30 percent of strippers and 24 percent of street-based sex workers who had been raped identified a police officer as the rapist.[1] Another approach that

---

[1] Raphael Jody and Deborah L. Shapiro, "Sisters Speak Out: The Lives and Needs of Prostituted Women in Chicago," Chicago Coalition for the Homeless, 2002 http://impactresearch.org/documents/sistersspeakout.pdf

is often suggested as a solution is the "Nordic model" that decriminalizes the selling of sexual services but criminalizes the purchase of them. Sex workers still have to deal with overpolicing and find ways that are safe for their customers to access their services without state surveillance. The goal shouldn't be to stop all sex work but to ensure sex work can be done safely because it will be done anyway. Sex work, after all, is the oldest profession, and all the efforts in many different human societies to stop it have never worked. It is not going away.

Decriminalizing sex work is what sex-worker activists are telling us they want. In fact, there are a growing number of sex-worker-led organizations, like Sex Worker Outreach Project, that are dedicated to supporting sex-worker human rights and educating the public, as well as policy makers, on decriminalization. It maximizes the legal protection of sex workers and actually decreases instances of human trafficking. It's important to make the very clear distinction between consensual sex work and human trafficking. Human trafficking refers to the use of use of force, fraud, or coercion to obtain some type of labor or commercial sex act. People who have been formerly trafficked are also in support of decriminalization as a way to better address trafficking. All sexual assault and human trafficking laws still apply under decriminalization too; there's just less legal confusion between the two. Again, for more resources on sex-worker rights, please check out the resources in the appendix.

When I stripped, I never met anyone I knew who was being trafficked. Traffickers generally don't try to mix their victims with consensual sex workers because we may figure out what is going on and try to help them. Which is not to say there weren't a few girls I worked with who didn't have controlling boyfriends who made me concerned about their agency, but the vast majority of the women I met were doing this work 100 percent willingly. I'm well aware I could've made other choices to deal with my grad student expenses, but I chose to strip and have no regrets other than not staying in the industry longer.

2004

1

I got involved with a former stripper before I ever became one myself. Lillian had gorgeous long red hair, tattoos, and wore glasses. She was working as a barista at a coffee shop in my college town, Champaign, IL. I was twenty-three and finishing off a year of fucking around partying before moving to Ann Arbor to pursue a Master of Science in Information at the University of Michigan.

One day, I went into her coffee shop and, as I often did when ordering things, I became annoyingly indecisive about what I wanted. "I want a green tea, or wait, maybe a chai... I think I'm hungry... I'm sorry I'm wasting your time."

Lillian just looked at me coyly. "Don't worry about it. I don't have anywhere else to be." I smiled and felt more at ease as she winked.

I finally picked a chai and enjoyed the feeling as her gaze lingered on mine while she handed it to me. Then another customer popped up behind me, and I realized I had to move along, but I knew I wanted to see her again.

Later, I found out from mutual friends that she was newly single and, like me, was hitting the bars like a fiend. We formally met when our friend groups started coalescing at all the local watering holes. After our drinking group finally reached critical mass, we declared ourselves a girl gang, named ourselves Pussy Control, after the Prince song, and convinced ourselves that we were a serious force to be reckoned with. Most guys quickly learned not to mess with us, because we would cackle at them or mock their ridiculous attempts to approach us. We were not the toughest or most organized gang ever, but we did at least manage to decrease the number of random guys hitting on us.

Maybe Lillian's risqué past was part of what drew me to her. I don't know. I had never thought there was anything wrong with stripping, but like most people, it was something I didn't think I would ever do. At the same time though, I was intrigued with her previous job and wondered what it was like to do something considered so socially deviant and potentially stigmatizing. I had actually done sex work before, but it was working as a dominatrix one summer in Chicago. That kind of work had its own stigma, but there was no audience, I didn't have to get naked, and I also didn't have to be nice.

Lillian would tell me about the stage and the pole tricks that would leave calluses on her hands. There were her quirky customers, like the man that just wanted her to sit still like a doll on his lap while he spoke to her. She explained how different customers liked different looks for their strippers and how she avoided working at clubs that only featured what she considered Barbie look-alikes. Lillian described living in Baltimore and how she would walk around half-naked all night, make good money, and then go home to her apartment. It sounded so normal, like being a waitress who happened to forget to put the rest of her clothes on.

Champaign only had one strip club, the Silver Bullet. I had been there once before. It was a dive bar that just so happened to have a small stage with a pole in the middle, as though it were a random afterthought. The lap dances were cheap and done on stools in an open corner of the bar. The girls didn't have a proper dressing room; they changed and did their makeup in the bathroom. Lillian had looked into working at that club when she first moved to town and decided against it after realizing she would end up bumping into random customers around town, so she had settled for a series of barista jobs while attending the local community college.

For a while, Lillian had talked about taking a trip back to Baltimore to see family and friends and make some money at her old club, which would solve some of her credit card debt problems. At first, she invited me along to work with her, and I was left with the question of whether I wanted to actually try stripping. The more I thought about it though, the more I felt sure I could do it. I would have someone to coach me and help me feel comfortable. I would also be in a strange city where I wouldn't have to worry about running into anyone I knew, and hopefully, I'd come home with a big pile of cash. If I wasn't happy with the experience, I could just leave it in Baltimore.

As the time for her trip got closer, we had started to grow more distant. She was beginning to gravitate toward a male bartender and making up weird excuses for why she had to hang out with him instead of me. She knew I was leaving town in two months, so I understood that. I also couldn't easily leave my waitressing job, nor was I really getting the incentive from her to try harder to get time off. So it looked as though maybe I wasn't meant to strip after all. Nonetheless, a stripping seed had been planted in my mind.

Later that summer, Pussy Control decided to surprise my friend Allison with a particularly outrageous night of alcohol and debauchery for her twenty-first. We started by putting all of our efforts into acting as though we were too busy or too thoughtless to care about her birthday throughout the day. Later on, we ambushed her and told her we were kidnapping her and she had to wear a blindfold. She happily went along with this plan, and we purposely drove her around in circles for a while, so she would have no idea where we were taking her.

We took the blindfold off in the Silver Bullet's parking lot, and she quickly realized where we were. She thought it was hilarious. We entered the small, dark, packed bar, and I checked out the one stage, which was a rounded rectangle that looked like a big Formica retro kitchen table. The men who were gathered around it all looked our way and managed to keep their gazes on us for a good portion of the night.

At first, I didn't understand why these men paid such inordinate amount of attention to our gaggle of fully clothed girls when the room was filled with almost-naked women offering to grind them for only ten dollars a song. At the time, it was flattering, if confusing, but after becoming a stripper, I understood that these men were going after the women who appeared to be more of a challenge, more of a mystery— but possibly sexually available, because why else would they be at a strip club?

At one point, a female customer who was not with our group got called onto the stage. We watched as two strippers sat her on a chair against the pole and handcuffed her hands behind it. They proceeded to mount her and bounce up and down, both of them facing her, with one upside down and hanging from the top of the pole. Then they whispered something in her ear and lifted her shirt up to the bottom of her bra. She began laughing, and the crowd went wild.

After that, I decided I had to get Allison on the stage for her birthday as well. I made my way to the bar and inquired about that, and the bartender pointed out the manager. He told me it was only ten dollars, so I paid him and wondered why it was so cheap.

That was easy enough. Allison was going up, and we were ready for it to be a riot. Not much later, they called her to the stage. As with the last girl, they handcuffed her around the pole and began dancing. This time, though, after one of the strippers whispered in Allison's ear, they lifted her entire shirt, revealing her breasts to the audience. The crowd went wild and began throwing money onto the stage. Allison looked shocked, but she was still laughing.

Then they pulled down her skirt, exposing her panties to the entire bar. She looked like she was beginning to feel uncomfortable but smiled anyway. I wasn't sure. I began to regret getting her up there. I didn't want to totally humiliate her, especially on her birthday.

The song ended, and the strippers helped Allison dress. When she came back to the table, I asked her how it was.

"It was fun. The strippers were very sexy," she said reassuringly.

"I swear I didn't know they were going pull your shirt up!"

"It's okay. They asked if they could do whatever they wanted, and I said 'yes.' I had a feeling they were going to do something like that."

I wasn't one hundred percent convinced, though. I knew I had a tendency to get carried away with a ridiculous scheme and not necessarily take into account the feelings of the other people involved. I was second-guessing myself. Allison was the type of person to be more concerned with reassuring others than with her own embarrassment, so it was obvious what I had to do. She couldn't feel bad if she wasn't the only one in our gang who got half-naked in front of a bar full of people, right?

I went back to the same manager and gave him another ten dollars. I was going onstage next. I might have just been paranoid, but either way, Allison was going to get my exposure solidarity. I was also about to have an absurd amount of fun.

As with the girls before me, the strippers sat me in the chair and handcuffed my hands behind me around the pole. The music started, and the same two girls who'd danced for Allison and the first girl began to caress me. I briefly wondered why they were the ones who always seemed to do this kind of stage dance. I wasn't going to complain, though—they were both very attractive.

One of them leaned in and whispered in my ear, "Can I pull your shirt up?"

I nodded, and the other girl proceeded to grind my lap. I was feeling the thrill all over as the other girl mounted me and began to bounce up and down. I felt a hand begin to caress my thigh. Fingers were slowly making their way up, and I got completely lost in the moment.

I had gotten so absorbed in the experience that I didn't notice what song was being played, but when it was over, the two girls dismounted me, and I finally began to notice the audience. The room was full of men who were obviously ogling me while my shirt and bra were still pulled up. That was the first moment I'd felt exposed throughout the whole process, and it wasn't embarrassing at all, just surreal. I'd definitely been looked at that way before in my life but never by so many men at once. It did feel a little awkward, but at the same time, I felt liberated. I'd broken a major social taboo about bodily exposure, and it really wasn't a big deal.

I looked down. Dollars were strewn about the stage. Even though I'd paid for the dance, the girls who performed for me appeared to make out quite well using me as a prop. I finally understood why those stage dances were only ten dollars. I didn't mind, but I had to admit I was a little jealous.

More and more, stripping began to float around in my mind as an increasingly viable option. I was entering a graduate school program that would require me to pay out-of-state tuition. I was under the unfortunate impression at the time that getting a degree from one of the best schools in the country would certainly ensure my future employment opportunities, especially if I wanted to work in an academic library.

I should have been more excited. I had gotten into a really good school. I knew I really wanted to be a librarian. It was the only English-degree career that had made sense to me. Once I had gotten the idea, everything seemed to fit. I could support research and remain part of academia without having to specialize. I had so many positive memories of being in libraries, as well as childhood fantasies of getting locked in one overnight. I had volunteered in my high school's library and wanted to work in one in college but ended up focusing on waitressing jobs because they paid more.

I was feeling good about my career choice, but not so much about the pathway I had picked to get there. I always knew I wanted to go to grad school, but part of me felt suffocated whenever I thought about the tuition bill I would have to pay off at the end of the program. In retrospect, it made absolutely no sense to attend a school that would leave me with a debt of $80,000 when I would ultimately be entering a low-paid profession like librarianship.

The University of Michigan School of Information, however, went out of their way to assuage my fears. They sent me bright materials with smiling alums describing their amazing jobs post graduation. Professors and current students emailed me repeatedly to see if I had any questions. I finally figured that this would work out somehow even though I didn't know what that way was yet. They wouldn't offer the degree if it didn't pay off in some way, right?

Looking back now, it's much clearer that I had better options. I could have reapplied to Illinois, or to Dominican University in River Forest, IL, and moved back in with my parents in the Chicago suburbs (online programs barely existed at this time). But along with being naive, I was also impatient, and I didn't want to wait any longer. I also didn't want to live with my parents again. Good or bad, I was convinced Michigan was the only choice available to me.

2

In July, a month and a half before I moved to Michigan, I broke my humerus in a random fall. The bone snapped completely in two, and I had to wear a heavy cast for several weeks, followed by an awkward brace that made me look like I was wearing football-player padding on one side of my body. My doctor told me that it would be several months before my arm felt normal again.

The broken arm had forced me to take a well-needed break from the bars and drinking. My two-month fling with Lillian had come to an end, which was fine. I needed to focus on my health and grad school plans.

At the time, I was waitressing and trying to save up money for living expenses during grad school. Needless to say, I was unable to work for the rest of the summer, which further dwindled my sad collection of funds.

My mom drove me up to Ann Arbor and helped me find an apartment. The cheapest two-bedroom apartment I could find was $800 a month—far more than I would have paid in central Illinois in 2004.

I posted ads on a University of Michigan housing website, looking for another female student to live with. I got plenty of emails and phone calls. I ended up giving more attention to the people who called, because in order to respond to email, I had to type one handed, and that just took forever when someone had a zillion questions about the apartment.

The first girl who called me sounded promising, but she got hung up on the fact that the apartment didn't have hardwood floors. The next girl who called got really weird when I asked her what she was studying. She said, "Psychology, but why should that matter?" I didn't consider it a personal question, especially between two people considering living together. So I told her I liked to drink a lot, and she quickly lost interest in my apartment.

The third girl who called wasn't that picky and didn't have a problem with my basic getting-to-know-you questions. Her name was Caroline, a chemistry PhD student who was about my age. We got along well on the phone, and I could glean from her that she liked to party, at least sometimes. At the time, that seemed pretty important to me. I didn't want to live with someone who was judgmental about having fun, because that was still my premier hobby.

That fall, I moved to Ann Arbor and attended orientation for my program within the next few days. The people running the orientation pumped us up to get us excited about learning the science of information. My program was one of a growing trend of schools dropping the word library to instead call themselves an I School. I think they wanted to be perceived as being on par with the B-Schools. The idea was that information science could be applied regardless of what field you were in. They emphasized their interdisciplinary nature and how you could do just about anything at the intersection of people, information, and technology.

There were four concentrations available at the time, and I technically started in the Human Computer Interaction track. I was interested in how people used technology, and I thought this would give me the opportunity to study that kind of interaction from an academic perspective. Then I could apply those skills later on while employed in a library setting. Part of the rhetoric of SI—the School of

Information—was that you could do any concentration and pursue another career track afterward because studying information was just that powerful.

The first semester was an eye-opener, though. My classes were filled with busy work and group projects focusing on information theory. I was younger than a lot of my classmates, and my immaturity was really obvious even to those who were closer to my age. They all took these classes very seriously, while I thought most of our assignments were silly and disappointing. I had an idealized idea of what grad school should be, and instead, I got a bunch of buzzwords thrown at me about how great information was. Few faculty members in the department were actually librarians, and there were few courses related to library work. There was one older professor whose focus was public libraries. I think she felt compelled to stick around because without her, there would be very little actual representation of libraries in my program. The other librarian-professor's focus was on databases and academic librarianship, and she proved to be pretty hard to get a hold of outside of the classroom. I don't think I ever got a reply from her via email.

I also had trouble getting the attention of my human-computer interaction professors. When we had our first advising session to plan classes for the second semester, I emailed my official advisor about when I could meet with him. He emailed back, instructing me to sign up on his door. I was in the building at the time he sent the message and received it right away, so I immediately wandered over to his office door. All of the advising slots were already full. I realized he was sitting in his office at the time and had probably known this before emailing me. That same man had sat with me during my informational visit and had emailed me a few times, to see if I had questions encouraging me to reach out, before accepting my admittance to Michigan.

I was also surprised to have classes taught by graduate student instructors. I thought as a graduate student I would have more access to my professors. Instead, we had PhD students leading our discussion sections, making it all the more clear to us that some of our research-oriented professors felt there needed to be a layer between us and them. The longer I was at Michigan, the more grad students I met from other disciplines, and none of them had GSIs teaching their classes.

My first two semesters included courses with names like Use of Information, Search and Retrieval, Social Systems & Collections, and Choice and Learning—all vague concepts with even vaguer assignments. We were told to write a paper about a collection, write about a time we were looking for information, get together and write about what it was like to search for information collaboratively, and then write about a time we searched for information for someone else. I tended to write the shorter assignments up an hour before class. I worked better under pressure, and with an English-major background, I found it easy to quickly generate acceptable papers that weren't really about anything at all. I always got good grades on these throwaway papers, which further convinced me that these were not legitimate assignments designed to help me learn something.

All of this really felt pretty disappointing. I was paying almost $20,000 a semester in out-of-state tuition and living expenses. I had managed to get a job with the University Library system, working at the Museums Library. I made $5.95 an hour. I really wanted to waitress somewhere, but I had to spend time working in an actual library so I could get experience before I graduated. I also wasn't ready to carry trays again because my arm was still healing. Even if I could use my arm, I wasn't sure how much time I would have to commit to being a full-time graduate student in my first semester and whether I would be able to work two jobs. So I continued to live off my loans, feeling more and more uneasy as I thought about the debt I was accumulating.

By the beginning of my second semester, I was still pondering the option of stripping, especially as my arm continued to heal. Whenever

I got overwhelmed with thoughts about how much money I had to pay back, stripping kept creeping back into my head as the most obvious solution. At the same time, though, I had also gained about twenty pounds because of temporarily quitting smoking. I didn't think I had enough confidence to succeed as a stripper, and I didn't know whether or not those twenty pounds were truly a detriment to moneymaking, but they felt like they would be. I couldn't tell if I was using the weight as an excuse or whether stripping really was a genuinely bad idea.

In March of that year, I went on the School of Information's Alternative Spring Break. This was a popular way for students to go on a trip but to a destination where the main purpose was helping out an organization through volunteer work. I had done something similar my sophomore year of college, when my group went to Minneapolis to help LGBTQ and HIV/AIDS advocacy groups.

This time, we were going to New York and being split up to "help" different organizations with their information needs. It was supposed to give us practical job experience, help us develop new skills, and benefit those groups with our free assistance. I had received my third choice on the application: the Poets House, which I'm not really sure why I selected because I have never been a very big fan of poetry. I was beginning to sink into depression and thought this trip might be a nice change of scenery as well as a way to bond with my classmates and perhaps finally make more friends in my program. I had clicked with the members of one of my group projects during my first semester. Thereafter, we always tried to get into each other's group projects in other classes we took together and occasionally hung out socially. Beyond them and a few coffee shop acquaintances, I hadn't really made many real friends in Michigan.

Yet I didn't end up making any new friends in New York City. We stayed in tiny YMCA rooms in the Upper West Side, and my roommate for the week took mercy on me and invited me to visit museums with her. One night, I went out with a big group and got inappropriately drunk. Other nights, I lay in my bunk bed with earphones attached to my laptop, watching TV shows on DVD and waiting for my sleeping pills to start working.

Two other women were assigned to the Poets House with me. One worked on some cataloging issues, and another worked with me to create a report about library architecture and shelving space. We found out later that the group from SI who worked at the Poets House the previous year had made the exact same report, so we were really just doing well-meaning busy work. During lunch hour, the woman who did the cataloging would invite my report partner out for lunch without me, so I wandered around Chinatown by myself. I could tell she didn't like me, although I didn't recall ever saying much in front of her, so I never really figured out what the issue was. By the end of the week, my architecture-report partner began inviting me along, but the cataloger made it difficult for me to include myself in the conversation. She'd probably picked up on my general negative and depressive energy and wanted to avoid me.

This should have been a fun time, but I wasn't feeling it. I found our project completely pointless while most of the other people had more positive and interesting experiences. By the time I came back from New York, I was ready to finally admit I was depressed. I was drinking almost every night and watching TV shows on DVD for hours until I fell asleep. I did the bare minimum required of me in order to be a functional person: I went to class, went to work, and did my homework. After that, I just wanted to escape.

Everyone around me seemed excited about their future careers in libraries and other information-oriented professions. Instead, I just felt like I was sinking. One day, I finally did the math: after subtracting the portion of my loans that were for living expenses and dividing my credit hours and how much time was spent in each class, I discovered that I was paying $300 for each three-hour lecture. I was angry at the

School of Information and felt like they were ripping me off, but I was angrier at myself for getting into that position in the first place.

By the time my second semester was ending, I was looking forward to just going home and staying with my parents for the summer. I needed to get out of Ann Arbor. The School of Information didn't offer any classes during the summer, so I couldn't stay and get more credits even if I wanted to. We were all supposed to get summer internships so we could gain experience to put on our résumés.

The types of internships they promoted were a mix of paid and unpaid. I had tried to meet with the School of Information's career advisor to get help searching for a paid internship that was either based in Chicago or Ann Arbor so I wouldn't have to pay for additional room and board for the summer. Considering my financial situation, it would be almost impossible to do an unpaid internship. I had sent the career advisor an email with all of my availability, which included several hour slots every day of the week for two weeks. She emailed me back saying she was busy and that I should meet with a second-year student who'd had an internship the summer before to discuss my search. At that point, I wasn't very surprised anyone in my program's administration didn't have time for students, so I went ahead and met with the student she'd suggested. I learned there were very few paid internships in libraries that were specifically for the summer, especially considering my geographical constraints, so I decided to just forget about it.

By the end of my first year, I knew that I was no longer interested in academic libraries. My job at the Museums Library wasn't bad, but it was boring. I had entered library science wanting to be part of academic culture and thinking that becoming a librarian was a good way to do that without having to specialize. I had begun to see though that academic culture might not really be for me after all. At heart I was probably too working class.

At the end of the day, I needed to feel that I was making a difference for people with more immediate needs than those in an academic setting. I didn't have much interaction with undergrads at the Museums Library. We usually just helped grad students and professors access materials. We were just doing administrative tasks related to other people's research. I realized I wanted to be helping people with greater needs find information and learn how to use technology, which made me shift my focus to public libraries. I already at least had the sense to understand that doing something that felt meaningful was one way to help get myself out of my funk.

It made more sense for me to get a job in a public library for the experience than to do an unpaid internship. So my plan became to find whatever work I could in a public library when I came back to school for my second year, even if it meant I had to start out by shelving books.

3

---◄O►---

I n the summer, I went back to my parents' house, still in a total
slump. I hadn't spent a summer there since I was twenty-one.
Previously, I had considered not living with my parents an
important part of growing up and feeling self-sufficient. This time, I
was twenty-four and depressed. Home seemed like the happiest place
I could possibly be.

I spent the first few days lying on the living room couch, watching
the last two seasons of Angel. The first thing I had done when I had
gotten back into town was drive around to local video stores to try to
find the seasons I had missed, but no one had as extensive a collection
of TV shows on DVD as the store in Ann Arbor. I could have ordered
them used on Amazon, but then I'd have to wait for them to arrive.
My irrational desire to escape wasn't able to accept that, though, so I
went to Borders and purchased them off the shelf for about one
hundred dollars altogether, which was a pretty stupid thing to do when
I had barely anything left in my checking account. I didn't bother to
actually check my balance. Instead, I did the math in my head and
figured I should have roughly eighteen dollars left, so it should be
okay.

After the days it took me to finish watching the series, I managed
to get up and start thinking about a summer job. I had no money left,
and I needed to seriously make some if I was going to make it through

the next semester. My first and favorite job prospect was an all-night Denny's I had previously worked at for four summers during college.

I also associated Denny's with happier times. I used to work until three or six in the morning, and when it wasn't busy, I would just sit around and chain smoke, hanging out with the regulars—a bunch of other listless teens and twentysomethings who didn't like sleeping at night either.

When I finally wandered into Denny's, my old manager was still there, and I was able to get a few dinner shifts to start with. My classes let out earlier than Illinois colleges, so I was able to beat out a lot of other college students looking for summer work, despite my initial inertia.

My summer started uneventfully. I wasn't making much money on three dinner shifts a week, and my parents were beginning to get on my nerves, but in a good way. I was starting to feel less disconnected, and that was what I needed. I went out with friends and tried to be more frugal. I was able to achieve a serious decrease in my drinking. Being around my parents also helped, because I didn't want them to see me borderline drunk all the time.

Eventually, I began to pick up more shifts on both dinner and overnight. Sometimes, I could stop in and convince one of the other servers to give me their shift. That was easy with the younger kids, who just wanted an excuse to go hang out with their friends instead of work anyway. At least they made me feel responsible by comparison. I got into a zone where I knew my main focus should be making money, and I tried not to think about what it would be like to go back to Ann Arbor in September.

Despite my dread at returning to school, I had to ensure my ability to continue financially at the School of Information. In the middle of June, I suddenly realized I hadn't applied for financial aid for the next school year. Although I had filled out a FAFSA every year throughout college, that step had completely failed to occur to me during the last year. Depression brain fog has a way of letting important tasks like that get completely missed.

I filled it all out super late and my application came back negative for my Perkins loan as well as for all of my private loans through Citibank. I was only eligible for federal loans. I had failed to get the Perkins loan because I hadn't applied in time. It was completely my fault, but I could still pay tuition without it—living expenses would be extremely tight, but I could do it if I secured more lucrative employment than working at the Museums Library when I returned to Ann Arbor.

I couldn't continue, however, without my private loans. I had received them the year before, so I didn't know what the problem was. My dad suggested checking my credit, which was something I had naively never considered before. I went online and figured out how to get my credit report. It turned out that two negative lines on my credit history had appeared within the last year. Overdraft fees, a recurring subscription I thought I had cancelled, and an unpaid medical bill had all contributed to bad credit—my inexperience with financial issues had made their mark. Despite efforts to rectify the problem, there was nothing I could do to fix it.

Until I tried to apply for financial aid, I hadn't understood what that had done to my credit history. In a way, this whole situation would have been better if my financial aid had been rejected the year before I tried to go to grad school. I would have learned early on that I wasn't really in the proper financial position to attend a school like Michigan, and that would have forced me to find less expensive ways to get a library degree.

In order to go back to school, I needed a cosigner on my private loans. I thought my parents would step up, but it took a lot of work persuading my dad to do that. I had to assure him several times that I would be responsible and someday pay the money back. I also attempted to tell him about my plan to be a stripper to make more money, which he just didn't even acknowledge as humanly possible. He thought it was ridiculous.

I had secured just enough money to return and complete my degree when I ran into one more literal roadblock. One night, I was driving home after hanging out with friends in Chicago and I was pretty tired. I can honestly say I hadn't been drinking that night. I do remember thinking it would be a good idea to stop and get an energy drink for the drive home, but I never actually pulled over to do so. During one dark stretch in a wooded area, a deer appeared directly in front of my car. I honked and tried to veer, but it was too late.

The saying "like a deer stuck in headlights" proved to be true. The deer didn't budge an inch and, as a result, bounced off my car. Naturally, I panicked, but my car was still running. It was dark and I just wanted to get home and see the damage, so I kept driving. It was only about five miles more to my parents' house at that point, but as I drove, I noticed that one of my headlights was out and that my steering fluid was leaking. By the time I pulled into my parents' driveway, I could barely turn the car.

The next morning, the mechanic quoted repairs at $4,000—my mom and I argued about the possibility of reducing the cost by using mismatching parts, something she didn't support because of appearances. I was starting to see where I had learned my unrealistic financial decision-making from. At the end of the day, my parents won the argument, and I ended up going out with my dad and spending the $4,000 on another used car rather than repairing the damaged one. This time, it was a '97 Saturn. I had to put a down payment on it with the money I had started saving from Denny's and take out another loan.

I didn't know how I was going back to Ann Arbor in the fall without finding a better job to supplement my loans. I also needed to try to find work in a public library that would allow me to get some relevant experience. So I began to think about stripping again. I had already considered going back into becoming a professional dominatrix, but there were no houses of domination in the metro Detroit area. All of the people who worked as pro-dommes were independent. I didn't feel like I had enough experience to go that route because I had only done it for a summer in Chicago when I was twenty. Then I'd had the guidance of a head mistress and the other women I worked with. Plus, I had access to an elaborate playspace and equipment.

I had only lost a little of my quitting-smoking weight before starting the habit again, though. At the time, I didn't feel comfortable trying stripping without shedding some pounds first. I began working out four days a week and watching what I ate. It felt good to have a plan, even though it sounded ludicrous to everyone else when I actually said it out loud.

I began to plan out other things I could do to prepare. All the strippers I had seen or imagined had big, long hair. Over the past year, as I had played around with the idea of stripping, I started growing my hair out from my college bob. Although my hair was very fine and thin, I was trying to keep it healthy enough to fling provocatively over my shoulder, or whatever it was I imagined strippers doing. I also went online and ordered aquamarine contacts.

I began visiting the tanning bed. I had always liked my pale skin the way it was, but I was getting into the idea that to become a stripper, I had to transform myself. The more I lived up to conventional definitions of beauty, the easier it was for me to believe I could assume that role. Beyond whatever other practical misgivings I had—and others that I probably should have had, such as the taboos associated with stripping—I was also worried about being attractive enough. I knew the first night would probably be terrifying. Being confident about how I looked was going to help.

I discussed stripping with some of my friends. No one fully believed me when I said I was going to do it. Everyone said it was outrageous and impractical. Most of my friends just laughed about it, but a few were seriously worried about objectification. They thought men would treat me like a thing, and as a result, I might begin to see myself that way instead of as a full, complex person.

For the second time in my life, I went to a strip club. This time, I went with a male friend to a club in the Chicago south suburbs. Going to a strip club with a guy was different from going with a group of laughing girls. It was easier to watch everything that was going on around me without also dealing with the gaze of the random men hanging out there.

I was able to observe this time how hard the girls were working. No one was showering them with singles just for being topless on a stage the way they did in the movies. They moved about the club, talking to different men sitting alone and in groups at the little tables. Some of them sat at the bar. I didn't know enough to wonder what the private dance area looked like or what doing private dances would entail at this establishment compared to the Silver Bullet. The private dance area wasn't visible to the rest of the bar like it had been at the Silver Bullet.

One thing I did take away, though, was that many of the girls looked very normal and had a variety of body types. I had yet to see an upscale gentlemen's club, and I appreciated that there were clubs women could work in without being perfect tens—whatever that meant. You didn't have to be stunning to be stripper.

At that point, my only obstacle would be not losing my resolve.

I returned to Ann Arbor at the beginning of September. Caroline had moved out to live in a nicer apartment. She had kindly invited me along, but I didn't want to deal with moving all my stuff. Plus, the rent there was higher and I needed to save every dime I could.

Since she had given me plenty of notice, I was able to secure a new roommate near the beginning of summer. I asked Aurora, a woman I had met my first semester in a group-project team at SI. I knew she hadn't been very satisfied with her first-year living situation and was debating on whether to stay. Aurora was eight years older than me and almost as immature as I was, so she'd agreed to move in.

Aurora had also not been satisfied with the School of Information curriculum, and already having the burden of loans from a private undergraduate degree, she decided to save money and transfer to Wayne State University in Detroit. She applied there as an in-state resident, and they accepted her without question, which significantly reduced her tuition bill to well under half of what she'd been paying before.

Aurora's decision definitely made me think twice. It was never too late to cut your losses, but part of me insisted I was halfway through and had to finish what I'd started, whether that made financial sense or not. I hadn't learned about the sunk cost fallacy yet.

I was also a little less embarrassed being a depressed drunk in front of Aurora than in front of Caroline, although Caroline had always handled it graciously. Aurora was depressed and dissatisfied with things in her own way as well, so we had that in common, though I had actually succeeded at reducing my drinking over the summer and was using valerian root to help with my insomnia more often than alcohol.

Things were beginning to feel a little more normal, which made me second-guess my stripping plans yet again. Shortly after going back to Ann Arbor, Aurora came with me to do more "research" at another strip club. I had been following online reviews of different strip clubs in the metro Detroit area, and so far, my first choice had been the Landing Strip in Romulus. It was one of a few clubs in the area with an airplane theme because it was located near the Detroit Metropolitan Airport.

We went early in the evening, around eight o'clock. This place was more upscale than the previous clubs I had visited and had actual decor. There were ivory columns and gold velvet curtains and roses on the carpet. The lights were brighter and the girls wore heavier makeup. Most of them looked pretty bored, though. I made a concerted effort this time to watch the girls as they interacted with customers.

We were surprised by how lackadaisically they performed onstage. Their bodies went through the motions of a slow, seductive dance, but their faces looked completely void of interest and some were tinged with annoyance. At first, I figured this was because it was early in the night and they were saving their energy for when it got busier. There was no one seated at the stage, so there was not much tipping going on to motivate them, either.

Most of the customers were in booths against the wall. Several girls stopped by a booth occupied by a young man. Their body language started flirtatiously, and he seemed receptive and flirtatious back. Then they got to the point where they had clearly asked him to come with them for a dance, using varying levels of coercion. He just kept shrugging but encouraging them to hang with him anyway. I watched this happen with girl after girl. It clearly wasn't a matter of waiting for the right girl to come along. He wasn't buying a dance from anyone, period.

I watched similar interactions at a nearby booth. Two guys were watching baseball on a flat screen by the bar. Several girls stopped by and visited with them for a few minutes each. The difference, though, was that these guys didn't seem to want to talk to any of them, which made me wonder why they were there to begin with. There were much cheaper bars to watch sports in. Strip clubs have covers, and their drink prices are inflated more than double.

These interactions made me realize how much harder stripping would be than just taking my clothes off and writhing against strangers. Beyond smiling and pretending to like someone, you had to seriously hustle. I wasn't much of a salesperson. That realization was beginning to defeat my confidence. I was an introvert at heart, and it was hard for me to be socially aggressive with new people.

While we were at the Landing Strip, a bouncer who came over and asked us how we were doing. He was a large fellow who mumbled, and Aurora and I had to ask him to repeat himself a few times.

I asked him, "What do you have to do to work here?"

"You need to get a dancer lice?"

"I'm sorry—a what?" I asked.

"A dance license."

"What is that?" I asked.

"Everyone has to have..." The rest of his words were mumbled.

Aurora and I just looked at each other in confusion.

Later on, I looked up more about the Landing Strip and discovered that there was a $180 dancer's card that anyone who wanted to strip in the city of Romulus had to purchase in order to work at one of their two clubs. That start-up cost was a bit annoying, but what really didn't sit well with me was that I would have to register with the city and put my information into a database. I didn't want my name associated with stripping in any type of official sense. This was supposed to be an anonymous venture that I could pretend had never happened if I needed to.

Later, experience taught me that the reason our friendly, incoherent bouncer was hovering so much was to make sure we weren't prostitutes. My questions and naive facial expression probably helped convince him that we were not out looking for johns. To deter prostitutes, many strip clubs do not allow women to enter as customers without a male companion.

My resolve wavered again. I hadn't been thinking about the hustling component to the job. I would have to flirt and be persuasive. I would have to smile at grumpy guys who weren't interested in me— or anyone else, for that matter. I would have to play the role of a sultry extrovert for hours on end, and that seemed like it would take a lot of emotional energy out of me.

The reality was, however, that I had significantly less money to live on that semester, and one way or another, I had to confront that issue if I wanted to stay in school. I knew that I should find a public library job first if I was ever going to get the experience necessary for getting a job when I graduated, but the need for money was more immediate.

I spent a few days wandering around Ann Arbor, applying for waitressing jobs.

I probably applied to twelve places over two days, and then I just couldn't put in any more applications.

I still had my ten-hour-a-week Museums Library job, where I made minimum wage, but it left me with ample free time because half the time I was there, I could work on homework. I also signed up to become a test subject with the university's psychology department, although most experiments didn't pay more than fifteen dollars at a time, and the opportunities tended to be sporadic. Still, the semester didn't really work out with my very low wage when I considered all of my unavoidable fixed expenses such as rent, car payments, and basic grocery staples.

I never heard back from any of the restaurants I applied to, and I finally figured it couldn't hurt to try the public library angle again, especially if there was nothing else out there for me. I knew all the websites that posted library job openings in the area, and I applied to the jobs I was qualified for, which were not many.

I also sent out cold emails to local library directors, introducing myself and asking if they had any positions open, a move that I later learned was a pretty serious risk in the library profession. I was willing to do anything and eager to get whatever type of experience was available. When I tell people in my profession this story, they are surprised I got away with it. But I was naive and figured that it couldn't hurt after my complete lack of success in any other job search. A few directors were nice enough to reply and tell me I could keep an eye on their libraries' websites in case a position opened in the future. Finally, a director from the Suburban Public Library responded and asked me to send my résumé. I was so inexperienced that it hadn't occurred to me to send it with my initial emails. The director asked me to come in for an interview because she had seen on my résumé that I worked at the Museums Library. One of her staff who was also in library school at Wayne State was an intern there, and I had just recently met her. I was lucky to have a personal connection.

During all that time, though, I had been lurking on a stripper message board online. It was subdivided into several sections, including one for hustling tips, one for talking about specific clubs, and a place for women who were new to stripping to get advice and feedback. I had a gazillion questions about dancing on the stage, shoes, hair, makeup, what to say to customers, what to bring with me, and how other dancers would treat me. I was encouraged by reading about the first nights of women like me who had succeeded. Learning about the types of problems many strippers encountered in their daily jobs-- nervousness, sore feet, difficult coworkers, tipping out to other staff, and customers who wanted more than the women were willing to offer—was eye opening. I ended up with a well-rounded view of the whole enterprise, and I appreciated the idea of having a network of supportive women. My perception was that many strippers could be highly competitive while in the club fighting for customers, but in an online forum, they were empathetic and encouraging.

When I first found the stripper message board, I was just doing casual browsing, but it became my daily habit to check new posts and follow the women's stories and the responses of their colleagues and online friends. I realized once again that the idea of being a stripper was not going away. At that point, my interest was about more than the money I needed—it was about following through with my plans and not being afraid. Fear was bringing back my depression. I had built the stripping plan up so many times, and it made me feel weak to put so much time and thought into an idea and then keep backing off. I liked to see myself as an adventurous person who didn't shy away from a new experience because I was afraid.

I was finally done with all the overintellectualized deliberation. Most strippers didn't put this much thought into getting onstage. Doing it one night didn't mean I would be required to keep doing it if I didn't like it. No one ever had to know, and I could avoid the stigma if I was careful. Stripping had become an itch that I needed to scratch, or I would always wonder if I could've hacked it. I just needed to go ahead and try stripping. It wouldn't be the end of the world if it sucked and I was bad at it.

Annoying the hell out of myself was what finally forced me to make a plan and carry it out.

5

---◆○◆---

I had to start by figuring out what club I wanted for my first audition. I had decided not to go back to the first club I visited with Aurora because of the whole dancer-card issue. I determined it would probably be best for my confidence if I started at more of a dive bar, like some of the other clubs I had visited—I realized I was just more comfortable in a working-class environment.

I liked the idea of dancing in Detroit because it would be a decent distance from my life in Ann Arbor and there were dozens of clubs to choose from. However, Detroit required an even more expensive dancer's card than Romulus—$350—and once again, there was the creepy database issue. A registry of who worked in strip clubs seemed invasive and just another way to control the autonomy of women just trying to get by. There was a club called Deja Vu Club Ypsilanti, but that was the next town over from Ann Arbor and definitely seemed too close.

I ended up making my decision by relying on reviews from different online strip club directories. I sorted through information posted by both strippers and customers. I wanted to start with a club that wasn't too fancy but was not described as a total hell pit, either. Some sites measured how high the fees were for dancers and how hard the girls thought it was to sell dances. There were also reviews that noted how much contact was expected at each club as well as the perceived dancer quality. Low contact wasn't an option in Southeastern Michigan, but some clubs offered more contact (also known as higher mileage) than others. I also didn't want to go to a club where all the women were perceived to be nines or tens in terms of appearance—I was just too intimidated.

Customer reviews gave me information about a club's cleanliness and general atmosphere as well as the experiences with the women. I was able to dismiss clubs that made it easy for customers to get more than just a normal lap dance on a regular basis. I had learned enough online to understand that it was not unheard of for girls to perform "extras," which meant offering higher levels of contact that pretty much meant sex acts. I understood that I would probably encounter those requests at some point, but I wanted to find a club where it wasn't typical or expected.

I ended up choosing Bogart's, which was about thirty miles away, a middle-tier club with better-than-average reviews. I reminded myself that I didn't have to stay there long term. I could completely give up stripping forever after my one night or try another club later.

After finally selecting the club, my next step was to choose a start date. I called Bogart's to ask them when a good time would be to come in for an audition, and they said any weekday except Tuesday was good, and it was generally best to arrive an hour before their shifts, which started at noon and seven o'clock at night. That worked for me. I already knew I only wanted to work in the evening, and it seemed a little overwhelming to start on a weekend night anyway. For my first night, I picked a Thursday in the middle of October.

I also had to plan out everything I would bring with me. I had learned from the stripper message boards that most girls brought dancer bags with them that they stored in lockers in the dressing room. Several had even posted lists of the types of things they generally included in their bag. I packed contact solution, my glasses, a makeup bag, lotion, a water bottle, a brush, hairspray, a locker lock, the outfit and shoes I planned to wear, and another outfit in case I decided I didn't like the first one. I have no idea what first-time strippers did before the Internet.

I knew that everything would be easier once I finally got the first night over and done with. I could keep reading about stripping and making plans, but those activities weren't going to mean anything until I got on a stage. When my starting day arrived, I was nervous and excited from the time I woke up. I had two classes earlier in the day and a shift at the Museums Library to help distract me. But as soon as I got home, it was all about getting ready.

My outfit was a black sparkly two-piece with a thong underneath the bottom piece. I put it on under my clothes, although I knew most girls just changed in the dressing room. I planned to wear a pair of black platform knee-high patent leather boots with buckles up the sides. They were from my goth club days and seemed appropriate for the situation. I felt more confident in severe, intimidating footwear.

My thin black hair went about halfway down my chest and was too flat and mousy for the look I had envisioned, so I wore a hairpiece that went over my high ponytail. It had lots of volume and hung down to the middle of my back.

I was shooting for a look I knew how to execute: dark and a little mysterious. Although I hadn't been doing as much in recent years, I had plenty of experience going to goth clubs and doing the whole dark, mysterious thing. I basically looked like a dominatrix but softer and less severe. It was the easiest stripper archetype for me to emulate. I felt too much out of my element attempting to do the naughty schoolgirl or the glamazon or the girly-lacy-lingerie look.

I put on layers of teal eye shadow, thick black eyeliner, and red lipstick. My one accessory was a rhinestone choker, and I finished it all off with some cucumber-melon body spray. I had read that some customers steered clear of girls with too strong a scent, because they didn't want to go home to their families smelling like perfume.

The drive to Bogart's was about fifty minutes during rush hour. I stopped at a liquor store on the way and bought some Jack Daniel's Country Cocktails. I left so early that I arrived in the Bogart's parking lot by five thirty. It was too early so I slumped down in my car and began drinking one of the cocktails to boost my confidence. I watched men drive up and come in and out of the front door and began to feel even more self-conscious. I finished the cocktail and chugged a second one. I began to worry that someone would notice me and try to come up to talk to me. I was on the verge of psyching myself out, and I even pulled out of my parking spot and drove around the parking lot twice before stopping and parking in a spot on the other side of the lot.

I finished the rest of my cocktail and reminded myself that the beginning would be the hardest—really just the first hour or two— and then it would get easier. I needed the reassurance that I was hired, and then I could go from there. A few minutes before six o'clock, I grabbed my dancer bag and made myself get out of the car and march to the front door.

I really wanted to just walk in and sit down for a while and absorb the environment before doing anything or talking to anyone, but I thought people would look at me strangely if I did that.

A bouncer was sitting at the front door and I told him I was there to audition. He directed me to a younger guy standing by the bar. Rather than looking around, I walked toward the man with as much purpose as I could gather.

The guy introduced himself as Russ the DJ and told me that he didn't do the actual hiring—the evening manager hadn't arrived yet— but he could get me started. He told me he needed to take my driver's license and social security card while I went to the dressing room to get ready. He would copy them somewhere in the back and give them back to me. That kind of terrified me, and I asked him what they did with the copies. He said they just went into a file and their main purpose was to prove that everyone was legally old enough to work there.

I hesitated for a second, but I knew my response would make or break whether I could do this. It was still significantly better than purchasing a dancer's card and having my name in a database, so I took a deep breath, pulled my driver's license and social security card out of my wallet, and gave them to him. Then I headed for the dressing room.

When I walked inside, there was a large lethargic older woman sitting on a stool by a big mirror with a bunch of hairsprays, lotions, and accessories next to her. She was parked in front of a tiny TV with bad reception, and she only looked at me for a second out of the corner of her eye before directing her attention back to the TV. I decided to just walk past her and continue to the back of the small room. I found a wall of lockers and a bench. There was one other girl back there who was looking for something in her bag. I had read so many stories about stripper locker room drama that I planned to be as nice as possible to the other girls but still keep to myself and stay out of anyone else's way.

Since my outfit was already on under my clothes, I didn't need to do any preparation other than lacing and buckling up my giant dominatrix boots. That was a time-consuming task, but I was able to consider my next steps as I methodically tightened all the different parts. When that was finally done, I took a few deep breaths and locked everything that didn't fit into my purse in one of the available lockers. It seemed that the longer I waited, the more likely the manager would be there when I left the locker room, and the sooner the suspense over whether I was hired would be over.

I stalled a minute longer by visiting the one bathroom stall, located across from the semicomatose lady. I realized she had to be the club's "house mom," a position I had read about. It was her job to watch our stuff and provide us with basic stripper accessories. I had also known a stripper who had complained about her house mom when she found out that the woman had been using the "tampon scissors" to cut up pieces of licorice for the girls who worked there. This house mom hadn't put out any food, so that apparently wasn't going to be an issue for me.

When I finally ventured out of the locker room, I took the opportunity to look around the club a little more. The bar took up most of one side of the room, and the other side had three stages, each with a girl on it. The middle stage was the largest and had more seats around it than the others, with several poles on the corners of its thick T-shaped floor. In between the stages and the bars were tables with more seats. The room was definitely not full. Closer to the front door was a wooden platform at the top of a small set of stairs, where private dances took place. The room had about a three-foot wall around it, so you could see the backs of the heads of guys getting lap dances as well as the gyrating girls mounted atop them. Not much of a private room. But I could see how its high visibility could be appealing to a customer who wanted a preview of what a private dance would look like.

Fortunately, I didn't have to find DJ Russ. He came up to me with his clipboard. "Mark still isn't here. He might not be in till a little later." He paused and handed me back my license and social security card. "You're not fat, so I'm sure you'll be fine. I'll just go ahead and put you on the roster. What do you want your stage name to be?"

"Jade." I had picked this name out ahead of time. Aurora had suggested it, and I liked the way it sounded.

"You can't use that name. We already have a girl named Jade."

Shoot. I didn't really have a backup name. I thought back to the other random names Aurora and I had talked about. We had gone off on a tangent about Greek goddesses, and I had paused on the muse Calliope. I clearly needed to choose a name that was more unusual. "Is Calliope available?"

"Huh. How do you spell that?"

I spelled it for him, and he wrote it on his clipboard. "Ok, have you danced before?" He looked up.

I was sure he could tell by the look on my face that I had not. I shook my head in what was probably a pretty pathetic way.

"That's okay. You'll be fine. The main thing is just to pay attention to when you're supposed to go onstage. What we do is a rotation. I go through everyone on the list in groups of three. I call one girl up to the main stage and the other two to the side stages. I play three songs, and you are supposed to take your top off by the middle of the second song. Each time I get to you again, you'll go to a different stage. Every hour, we call a finale, and all the girls who aren't giving dances go up onstage at once. Any type of music you like?"

"I'm fine with whatever." I figured he wouldn't have the music I liked, and it seemed too complicated to try to explain. "Not country." I shrugged.

"That's fine." He nodded. "We don't play much country anyways. And no rap. The owner wants us to play mostly rock and roll." He showed me his clipboard again. "Also, make sure you pay attention to when you are on the main stage. We can skip you for the side stages if you're giving someone a dance, but not for the main stage, so finish up before I call you onstage."

A girl came up to interrupt us and asked DJ Russ for the clipboard. "Hey, Mercedes," he said as she signed her name.

I saw that I was third on the list. "So does that mean I'm going up in the first group?"

"I can put you farther down the roster if you like. We'll have plenty more girls in here before the shift starts at seven. You will have to go on when we do the finale at the beginning of the shift, though. All the girls go up there for a song as we switch from day to night shift. We can consider that your audition. Mark should be here by then…"

"Okay." That didn't sound too bad. I did like the idea of having my first time onstage be with a bunch of other girls. That really helped take the pressure off. If I ended up doing anything asinine, it would be easier to just blend in and hope no one noticed.

"And one more thing. The stage fee is seventy dollars a night, but you can pay sixty dollars if you pay when you come in. Since it's your first night, we can keep it at sixty dollars, and you can pay it later when you've made the money. Also, at the end of the night, you have to tip me out at least ten dollars, five dollars for the bouncer, and five dollars for the house mom. Any questions?"

"So just wait till seven, then go up onstage for a song and come back and check with you?"

"Yep, that's pretty much it." Two more girls came up to sign their names on DJ Russ's clipboard, and he began talking to them.

I went ahead and took a seat at a nearby table. It was only about twenty minutes till seven. I figured I would just sit there and try to get further acclimated. I had read about the house fees online but hadn't really considered how they worked in practice. Most clubs considered strippers independent contractors, not real employees, so that was how they were able to get away with charging a fee to work there. It was a standard practice, and according to online reviews, Bogart's charged lower fees than a lot of other clubs.

Everything seemed okay, but it was still a little unclear on whether I was hired and what the manager's role was in this. I would later learn that it was common for the DJ to do most of the actual managing at some clubs. I also wanted the reassurance that the fact that I wasn't fat was really good enough to seal the deal. And also, wow, was that a ridiculous hiring criterion.

I had watched enough stage sets before to not be surprised by what I saw. Some girls were slow and sexy. Others danced more athletically and made use of the poles for basic spins. And some just got on the ground and shook their butt cheeks—the original twerk.

Overall, there were fewer smiles than I thought there would be, but that changed whenever a customer came up to the stage to tip. I kept telling myself that it didn't look too hard, as I waited for the DJ to announce the finale.

More girls had continued to come into the club during this time, and I watched them go into the dressing room and go up to DJ Russ to sign in. I thought about getting a drink from the bar. The weak Jack Daniel's cocktails were not doing much for me at that point, but I figured I should at least wait until I actually got started before drinking more alcohol.

Finally, the voice over the speaker called the finale for the day shift. All the girls who had been working the floor got onstage and quickly took their tops off or just pushed them aside. There were at least twelve girls on the stage and a few still in the private dance room. As a group, they did not seem super excited, but I supposed that made sense since their shift was almost over. I told myself I would reward myself with a Long Island Iced Tea if I just got this first stage thing over with.

DJ Russ's voice overtook the speaker—the previous voice must have been the day DJ. Russ told all night-shift ladies to get onstage. I was sitting very close and could easily have been one of the first ones on if I'd wanted to. I was quite happy to let the other girls go first. Most of them trickled out of the dressing room and walked confidently onto one of the stages. I waited until it would be weird to continue to just sit there by myself, and then I finally climbed up.

It was surprisingly easy. I didn't feel much pressure to smile and act seductive because not that many of the other girls were doing that. Overall, the feel was routine and perfunctory. I just hung onto one of the poles and swayed a little. I really didn't notice what the audience was doing—I was looking mostly at the other girls. When I pulled my top aside, it felt like a total nonevent. And then the song was over just like that. I didn't even remember what had been playing—just another generic rock song that had come out sometime in the last twenty years and that I would probably hear played again another fifty zillion times throughout my stripping career.

When it was over, DJ Russ's voice went over the speaker again, announcing that Candy would be performing on the main stage. That was our cue to get off. I discovered that there was a more convenient little stairway on the other side of the stage, where one girl had volunteered to help the other girls climb down in their heels.

I wandered back to the DJ booth and stood there self-consciously. DJ Russ looked at me as if he didn't know why I was there.

"So is everything all right? Should I go talk to the manager?"

He shrugged. "Yeah, you're fine. He didn't say anything."

"Oh, okay."

"I put you near the end of the list." DJ Russ showed me the clipboard "And you'll start on a side stage. Sound good?"

"Yeah, that's fine." So I had gotten hired by not being vetoed. That was an unexpected approach, but I wasn't going to complain.

I wandered over to the bar, wondering who the manager actually was.

The bartender came up to me and took my order. "You know you can get customers to buy your drinks for you?"

I didn't want to tell him I was still working up to the customer part. "Oh, yeah. That's okay."

"And don't forget that if the waitress comes over and the customer wants to buy you a drink, you always have to say yes. That's part of how the club makes their money. You can always dump it somewhere later if you don't really want it."

I had encountered that common rule on the stripper message board, but it was good to be reminded. I took my Long Island Iced Tea and parked myself at the table I had previously been sitting at. It was funny how easily I'd developed a routine that made me more comfortable. The shift was seven hours. I figured I could afford an hour or two of just sitting there before trying to go talk to customers and get lap dances.

That would be the most challenging part. I looked around the room. Plenty of girls were already talking to the customers distributed around the bar, whose reactions varied widely. Some guys looked interested, and others looked bored as they tried to chat back politely. I didn't want to go up to one of these bored-looking guys. If they were bored with another girl, they would probably be bored with me too.

Eventually, a pretty young brunette stripper came up to my table. She almost smiled and then just sat down next to me. She was tall and wore a pink plaid bikini top and matching skirt. I expected her to say something, but she just stared blankly ahead and chewed her gum, so I decided to start a conversation.

"It's my first day. How long have you worked here?" I asked.

"Only a week." She shrugged.

"Is this your first club?"

"Yeah. It was my boyfriend's idea to start once I turned eighteen. He said I could make good money." She sounded so young. This was probably her first job of any kind.

"My name is Calliope."

She looked at me in a funny way and chomped on her gum. "Ca-*what*?"

"Calliope," I said more slowly.

"Oh." She looked as if that still didn't make sense. "I'm Jenny."

"Is that your stage name?"

"Oh, nah. I'm just using my real name. It's easier that way."

We sat there a while longer. I didn't seem to have much in common with this girl, but she was the first person to actually talk to me outside of DJ Russ, so as far as I was concerned, we were new best friends.

Randomly, she announced, "I'm really stoned."

That made a lot of sense. "Does that make it easier to dance?" I continued to sip my Iced Tea.

She shrugged blankly. "I just like to smoke. Me and my boyfriend smoke all the time."

I couldn't resist. "What does he do?"

"Nothing right now. He says he's not good at going to work every day. You know, following a schedule and all that."

"So do you like it here so far?"

"Yeah, it's okay. I can only smoke so much before I get here, though, or it's kind of hard to talk to people." Jenny paused. "Like, now I think I need to come down a little. I'm gonna smoke so much when I get done tonight." She almost brightened, but her overall demeanor remained lackluster. I wondered what she would talk about with customers. But she was so young and new and clearly preoccupied by pot—she probably didn't really have a plan for that. At least I wasn't the only one who didn't know what she was doing.

We sat there in silence for a while. DJ Russ continued to call more girls up to the stage and I watched their sets. I finished my Long Island Iced Tea.

Jenny asked me, "Do you smoke?"

"Sometimes, but not that often anymore." This was all Jenny wanted to talk about apparently.

"I like to smoke all the time," she stated matter-of-factly.

The song ended, and over the speaker, DJ Russ's voice broke out. "Thank you, ladies. And now to the main stage, Jenny, with Claudia and Kiwi on the side stages."

"Huh, that's me." Jenny giggled. She grabbed her purse and made her way to the stage.

I was sitting alone again. Somehow, sitting with someone else had made me feel as though I was sort of doing something. I wondered if I could eventually get in trouble for just sitting there and not doing anything. Then again, this Mark guy didn't seem like a very hands-on manager, considering that I still had no idea who he was. There were a few guys watching a football game at the bar. Maybe he was one of them?

I scanned the room again to try to gauge if I was ready to go try to talk to someone yet. I decided I would talk to someone at least by the time I finished my first stage set. I was hoping that once I was onstage, I would get a good look around and maybe know who might want a dance from me by who came up to tip.

As I made eye contact with the man at the table next to mine, I smiled shyly and continued to look around the room. I had been staring ahead so intently I hadn't realized anyone was sitting next to Jenny and me.

When my eyes scanned back past him, he began to pull himself up as if he was trying to get my attention. "Can I get a dance?" he asked timidly. He was a pretty big guy, probably not much older than me.

"Oh, sure," I said, probably with a little too much surprise in my voice. This seemed be perfect. I didn't have to hustle for my first dance and he seemed polite and slightly nervous.

I stood up, and he followed me to the private dance room. I went up the stairs and opened the little gate that separated the platform from the rest of the club. I really wanted to act as though I knew what I was doing.

"What's your name?" the big bouncer sitting at the gate door asked me. He had long black hair in a ponytail and looked a little like Danny Trejo. Like DJ Russ, he had a clipboard.

"Calliope."

I got another funny look. "And how do you spell that?"

I spelled it for him, and he wrote it down. The bouncer then looked at my customer. "Ten dollars for a wristband."

The man pulled his wallet out and handed the money over. Then the bouncer tied a florescent paper strip around his wrist.

There were already four or five dances going on in the oddly shaped room. I walked over to the clearest area and gestured toward a chair. The customer nodded and sat down.

"We can start when the next song begins." I set down my purse beside us. I had already learned that it was hard to count how long your dance was if you didn't do it song to song. So far, I was pretty confident I sounded as though I knew what was going on. I smiled and sat close to him and tried to make conversation. "Have you been to Bogart's before?"

He shook his head. "This is my first time."

Did he mean first time getting a lap dance? I wondered if I should I tell him it was my first time too. Probably not. The current song ended, so I stood up and began leaning against him. Most of the other girls had straddled their customers and were basically just bouncing on them. This guy was pretty big, though, so I ended up straddling one of his legs and trying to move sensually up against him.

I took off my top and caressed the skin behind the back of his ear. He had already seated himself on his hands, but that didn't appear to be the standard in the rest of the dance room. I turned around, facing away from him with my butt moving up and down on his thigh. I could observe the other dance pairs then and saw just how handsy some of the guys were. The bouncer seemed indifferent, so this behavior was clearly fine here. I really had gotten lucky with my first customer.

As with my first time onstage, the song was over faster than I thought it would be. I was a real stripper now. I turned around and asked him how his dance was.

He nodded and said it was good. I put my top back on and grabbed my purse. He stood up and handed me twenty dollars.

"Thank you." I walked out of the dance room and back to the table. I was beginning to feel really proud of myself until I realized I had completely forgotten to ask him if he wanted another dance. I had felt such a victory by just giving a lap dance that it hadn't occurred to me at the time to try to keep him going. That was what you were supposed to do—try to get at least a few songs with each customer. It was the best way for the money to add up. I felt kind of stupid. He was already out of the dance room at that point, and it seemed sort of ridiculous to go ask him if he wanted another.

I was clearly not a pro yet, but at least I had gotten started. I looked at my watch. It was only eight thirty. There were five and a half hours left.

6

DJ Russ's voice came over the speaker again. "Thank you, ladies. Will Diamond please go to the main stage with Angel and Cal... Calli-Op on the side stages." I figured that was me and I should probably touch base with DJ Russ about how to say my name. Then again, it hadn't been well received by anyone so far.

I liked the idea of starting my first stage set on the side stage. I had already watched almost all the girls working that night do their stages and very few performed with the acrobatic wonders you saw in movies about strippers. I had discovered that you really could just stand there and sway and swing slowly from the pole. Most girls did the slow-and-sensual thing. I already felt confident that I could do that and manage to keep a very bored expression off my face at the same time. I had already seen several girls who weren't getting any attention, looking out with completely spacey, uninterested expressions.

I wasn't ready for a confident smile, but I tried to at least give a shy smile as I moved around the pole. I had seen too many strip club customers online complain that they didn't want to approach or tip frowning strippers who looked as though they didn't want to be there.

Two guys were seated at the side stage I was on. One was looking away, for the most part, watching the Lions on one of the TVs above the bar. That would have been discouraging, but I had observed him doing the same thing most of the night. None of the other girls had been dazzling enough to really take his attention away, so it was okay if I wasn't either. I still didn't understand the sports-watching phenomenon in a strip club.

The other guy tipped me twice, which seemed more promising, although I had seen him do the same for the other girls who had danced on that stage. A few had stopped to talk to him afterward, but he did not go with them to get private dances. With my lack of experience, I didn't feel particularly confident about trying for a private dance after watching much more experienced girls get shot down.

The third song of my stage set was beginning to wind down. The football fan finally turned around and gave me a dollar as though he were fulfilling an obligation. I took it and thanked him. Then I put my top back on and climbed off the stage. The next girl DJ Russ had called up had already climbed the stage, and the tipper was now paying attention to her.

Now what? I thought. I decided to go visit the dressing room and check on my makeup. The house mom was still seated in a semiconscious state on her stool. I reapplied my lipstick and fiddled with the phony pony on my head. It was clipped into my real ponytail and felt as if it was sinking on my head. I brushed it out a bit and walked back out to the bar.

Jenny was sitting at the table we were at before. I went ahead and sat back down by her since we were new best friends and all.

I thought about asking her if she had gotten any dances, because I hadn't seen her when I was onstage, but I wasn't sure if that would go against some type of stripper etiquette. I had seen several girls post online that it was never a good idea to talk about your money with the other strippers in your club.

I was becoming conscious that I should be trying to wander around the bar and talk to customers. I had only made twenty-five dollars so far. The pressure had been off for the first hour or so because I was so concerned with acclimating myself. Now I had to begin thinking about hustling.

Suddenly, a customer came up to us. "Can I sit with you ladies?"

"Sure," I said. My reaction skills were faster than Jenny's apparently.

"My name is Chad. What are your names?" He was an average-looking guy with a white T-shirt that had the word *California* spelled out by silhouettes of naked women posing as letters.

He seemed to be looking at Jenny more than me, and that made sense. She was very pretty, and I knew I couldn't compete with her in the looks department.

"I'm Jenny."

"I'm Calliope."

"Never heard that one before," Chad said politely. "So what are you ladies doing tonight?"

Jenny looked at him blankly. It was up to me to make the small talk. "Not a lot. It's my first night here." I had read on the stripper message boards that some guys totally dug the new-girl thing. Plus, in the moment, I couldn't think of anything else to say.

"Oh, cool. First night here? Or first night stripping in general?" Chad asked raising his eyebrow.

Clearly, I would be playing the ingenue. "First night stripping in general," I said as coyly as I could.

"Ah, so what do you think so far?"

It's scary, and I have no idea what I'm doing. "Oh, it's pretty fun. Definitely different from other types of jobs I've had."

"Well, you can take it from me—I've been to a lot of clubs, so I know a lot about stripping." Chad went on to describe some of the clubs he'd been to around the country. Then he began discussing his T-shirt and how he had gotten it in a club somewhere around San Francisco.

At that point, Jenny joined in the conversation, probably realizing she would have to chat if she wanted any dances from Chad. "I've only been here for a week."

"Oh, cool. So you're both new."

One of the waitresses came over and asked him if he wanted anything to drink. He ordered another beer, and then she asked him if he would like to get anything for the ladies. Chad looked at us expectantly.

I remembered the rule about always ordering something. "I'll take a Long Island Iced Tea," I said, and Jenny ordered an energy drink called Sum Poosie. It was clear that Bogart's wasn't going to let underage strippers order alcoholic beverages on the premises. It was kind of funny that they were old enough to get naked and grind strangers but still not old enough to legally drink a beer.

When Jenny's Sum Poosie arrived, we examined the bottle. It just had a picture of a sexy lady on it, and the soda itself was hot pink. They were $6.50 a bottle and they were a strip club staple. There were many strippers under twenty-one, and plenty of girls who just didn't want to drink alcohol at work. Asking for "Sum Poosie" sounded better than ordering a Coke.

Jenny let me try her Sum Poosie. It tasted like any other energy drink.

"Now, that's a strong drink," Chad said, referring to my Long Island Iced Tea. He seemed to like the idea that I was doing some serious drinking.

"It should be a strong drink," I said. "I already had one earlier, and barely felt it. I have a high tolerance, though." I didn't want him to get the idea that I was going to get sloppy drunk really fast.

We talked a little more about our backgrounds. Chad was actually from Ohio, but he was in the area on Thursdays to teach a class in a manufacturing technique that I didn't really understand. Since it was the last day of class, he thought it would be a good idea to take the guys out to a strip club. They were seated at another table. "They're kind of cheap, so it looks like I'm going to have the most fun tonight."

I explained my background story. I already knew I was not much of a liar, so I had decided I would just tell customers the truth about myself while avoiding some of the more specific details. I told him I was a graduate student at the University of Michigan, studying to be a librarian. I didn't go into the fact that being totally broke was my motivation for pursuing this new profession, though.

"Ah, so double life, huh?" he said, raising his eyebrows again.

"Yeah, I needed to get out and have more fun." As if there were no other ways for a grad student to let off some steam besides becoming a stripper. "It's kind of exciting. I'm not going to tell anyone at school."

"I don't think I've met a librarian before. That's pretty sexy. So you like to read a lot?"

"Yeah." I nodded. My burgeoning stripper instincts told me to probably avoid letting the conversation get too bookish.

"That's hot. Want to give me some lap dances now?"

I brightened. "Absolutely."

"I'll get some dances with you too in a bit," Chad assured Jenny, who nodded indifferently.

We walked back to the private dance room and Chad and I sat down to wait for the beginning of the next song. When it began, I was able to mount him more confidently than my first customer—his smaller lap made it easier for my short legs fit around him.

"I can play stripper trainer," he said excitedly as I began to gyrate.

Oh boy, I thought. But Chad's instructions actually ended up being helpful. He told me to turn around and arch my back more—he wanted me to caress his neck and let my hair fall in his face a lot. At first, it was hard to find enough to do to keep a guy entertained for song after song, but I just did the same moves over and over and changed the order.

Chad got five songs altogether, and he was less handsy than some of the other guys receiving dances. He handed me one hundred dollars and then added twenty dollars as a tip and said, "I don't usually tip extra, but since it's your first night, I'll give you this."

At the time he sounded self-righteously benevolent about giving me the extra twenty dollars. But it would turn out that he was right— not too many guys paid more than they had to when buying lap dances.

We went back to our table, and Jenny was still sitting there, staring off into space. Chad began bragging about his stripper-training skills when one of his manufacturing students stopped by. He suggested that this guy get a dance with me, but the student declined.

"I told you those guys were cheap," he said when his student had left the table.

Chad finished the rest of his beer and asked Jenny to go for some dances. They went to the private dance room, and I continued to nurse my Long Island Iced Tea. I was finally beginning to feel the liquor, and my overall confidence was increasing. I didn't mind Chad's stripper-trainer bit because I really didn't know what I was doing. I could have run into a more ill-intentioned "stripper trainer" who would try to take advantage of me. Chad hadn't pushed anything inappropriate, or at least not by strip club standards.

That was the moment I became sure I could do the job. I had already made some money, and I still had half the night to go. Although I hadn't been able to go up to customers yet, I had still managed to get some to come to me. I was an introvert, but I had demonstrated that I could still pique a guy's interest by just talking to him. Jenny was prettier than me, but her complete lack of basic conversation skills had helped my cause.

Chad and Jenny came back after a few songs. He had paid for less time with her than me. She remained unexpressive, and I wondered if she really was that uninterested in everything. Soon after, she performed on the main stage and was tipped well by several guys.

Chad looked up at her, and then he looked back at me, "You girls are both really beautiful, but you know the difference between you two?" He paused. "You have that something else. I mean, Jenny can get there, but you can tell she's still really young."

I just nodded and smiled. I already knew I didn't want to speak negatively about the other girls in the club. I would soon learn how common it was for customers to compare a stripper to the other girls she worked with. For many of them, it was a way to give a compliment.

We chatted some more about why Chad liked strip clubs in Michigan more than Ohio. They were just more fun, he explained. From my observations of the stage rotation, I knew I would be up on the main stage soon.

As I walked up the steps, I did feel a little flutter in my stomach. Despite all the random flat screens showing sports, I would be the main focal point of the room. Maybe it was better to remain expressionless like Jenny, which might be easier to pull off than fighting the urge to make an *Oh my God, everyone's looking at me right now and I'm supposed to act sexy* expression. Until I actually had to do it, I hadn't realized how different dancing on the side stage and the main stage would feel.

I managed to kind of curl my lip up and keep it in a sort of semi-smile as I grabbed the pole and began leaning against it. If I had just known some pole tricks, that would have been a good way to distract myself from looking out into the audience, but with my limited experience, actually swinging around the pole would've been a pretty foolish thing to try to do.

I did feel somewhat confident that I had rhythm. At least I wasn't making any of those weird jerky movements characteristic of someone who didn't know how to dance. By the end of the first song, despite the urge to stare at the ceiling, I managed to scan the audience. Chad was smiling up at me, which made me feel a little more at ease.

The second song started and I took off my top. Once again, it felt like no big deal and, if anything, it gave me a little confidence boost about what I was doing. I began making brief eye contact with the guys in the audience I found looking at me. This time, I had more people looking at me than when I was on the side stage.

I looked down at some of the guys sitting at the stage and realized two had pulled dollars out. I went to the first, took my tip in the side of my thong, and moved on to the next one. I got back on the pole with a brighter smile, and a few more guys approached my stage with tips, including one guy with a five-dollar bill.

Finally, the last song was nearing its end and Chad had come to the stage to tip me. As I took my tip, he made sure I knew he wanted to get some more dances with me.

"And that was Callyoop," DJ Russ said. "Next up is Morgan." I put my top back on and descended the stairs. From the number of guys who had tipped me onstage, it seemed that I could probably get some dances if I went over and talked to them. But I liked the security of going back to Chad's table and knowing what to expect.

We went back to the private dance room, and I did four more dances with him. Afterward, he bought me one more drink—this time, I decided to go for just a beer. As it was getting late, I figured I didn't need that much more alcohol. Eventually, Chad thanked me for my company and told me he needed to drive back to Ohio and that he might stop by again sometime. I told him to have a good night and that I'd had a good time hanging out with him.

He had become something of a security blanket by that point, but I knew it was time to move on and try to talk to other customers. I looked around for the guy who had tipped me five dollars. He had seemed like a promising potential customer, but I didn't see him anywhere on the floor. He might have ended up finding another girl and getting dances with her. I looked at some of the other guys who had tipped me. They were sitting with other girls or were seated directly at the main stage, paying attention to the girl up there. There were still a few guys seated alone, but I realized I still didn't yet have the confidence to go up to them let alone the ones with other guys. Approaching a group was particularly intimidating. I grabbed a seat at the bar, reassuring myself that I wasn't doing too badly. I could be sociable—it was just so much easier if someone else started the conversation.

I looked at the time. It was eleven thirty. I had about two and a half hours left. I did some people watching until a man abruptly approached me and said, in a thick accent, "I want a dance with you."

"Sure thing." I smiled and got off my stool, but the man had already walked away briskly and was headed toward the private dance room. I scurried to catch up with him and followed him in. I sat down next to him to wait for the next song to start and tried to make conversation, but I received mostly grunting noises when I told him my name and asked him how his night was going.

When the song started, the man pretty much grabbed me by the sides and began bouncing me on top of him vigorously. I pulled back a little and tried to slow him down—it seemed that I should be the driver here. Eventually, he began taking over again and resuming his energy. I got that a lot of lap dances consisted largely of dry humping, but this seemed a little much. When the song was over, I reluctantly asked him if he wanted another and was relieved when he said no and handed me my twenty dollars.

I probably should have felt a little more offended by that experience, but that was just not where my mind went. I was already developing the detachment required to deal with those kinds of situations—that was what went with the territory of being a stripper, and I knew it was what I had signed up for. I was still glad that the guy had not been my first customer, though. I really don't know how different my stripping experience would have been had I started the night out with him.

Not too much more happened the rest of the night. I went on the side stage one more time and ended up sitting with one more customer for a while. He had tipped me earlier, and I went up and asked him if he would like some company—I had finally proved to myself that I could approach a customer. I picked him because he seemed especially congenial, but he did not end up having that much money. He bought me a soda and gave me a few more tips but ended up sheepishly explaining that he did not have enough money to buy dances. I made conversation with him anyway, and he told me about his job at Home Depot.

Before I knew it, DJ Russ was calling the grand finale of the night. Every girl was supposed to get onstage. I wasn't quite sure about the purpose of everyone getting up, because at that point it wasn't possible to buy any more dances unless you were already with a girl in the private dance room.

I looked around at the other girls. Most of them didn't actually bother to take their bikini tops off but just pushed them to the side. The indifferent look that I had seen on the faces of Jenny and a few of the other girls had become much more common. Everyone just wanted to go to the locker room to change their clothes and go home.

When the song was over, I went up to DJ Russ and paid my sixty-dollar house fee and gave him his ten-dollar tip. Mentally, I calculated how many girls were working and how many had given him at least ten dollars—that didn't seem like a bad deal. I assumed the club had to also be paying him an hourly wage since he was on a schedule, unlike the strippers, who were contract workers.

I found the bouncer and gave him five dollars and then went to the locker room, where the house mom had perked up just enough to make sure she got her tips from all the girls coming in the door. It was pretty crowded, so I carefully ducked and scooted by several other girls to get at my locker and gather my things. It occurred to me that it probably would have been nice to quickly pull on some clothes and go as some of the other girls did. But I had to sit on the floor and untie my elaborately sealed boots.

So far, none of the other girls had talked to me, and I had managed to slip in under the radar and not step on anyone's toes. I quietly counted my money and found I had made $170. That wasn't too great but was probably good for my first night when I hadn't really attempted to hustle yet. It also felt good to finally make some money after making minimum wage at the Museums Library.

I left the locker room and headed to the parking lot, which was being guarded by the big bouncer. I figured he was probably there to keep customers from lingering too long or trying to talk the girls into getting in their cars.

I was happy to head home. It would be about a forty-minute drive at two o'clock in the morning, and I couldn't wait to crawl into bed and go to sleep. My eagerness to get home, however, got me pulled over in a speed trap only a mile from my apartment.

It was the middle of the night, and I was coming home from working as a stripper. Now I had a cop approaching my car. Although it had been several hours since I'd had a drink, I knew I had alcohol in my system.

I was kind of a pro at getting pulled over, so I quickly got my license, registration, and proof of insurance ready for the officer before he even got to my window. My experience in these matters also allowed me to exude as much compliance as possible. That must have impressed him enough to not inquire about what I was doing that night or where I was coming from. Of course, I'm sure the fact that I was white also likely helped shield me from further scrutiny.

Eventually, he told me that he was going to do me a favor and write me a ticket for going ten miles an hour over the speed limit instead of how fast I was really going. I thanked him and asked him how much it was.

"I don't know. You're going to have to look it up when you go to pay it."

"So you don't know how much I'll need to pay? Even an estimate?"

"Like I said, I don't know," he replied in an annoyed voice. "You can find out if you go to the website on the back and put your ticket number in. It should show up in a day or two."

"Okay." I wasn't thanking him this time. Wanting to know how much I was being fined seemed perfectly reasonable. It was pretty unprofessional to be handing out tickets without at least telling people how much they were going to be required to pay. I'd had my fair share of moving violations, and every other cop who had pulled me over had no problem giving me this information.

The officer walked back to his car and I was free to go. My surprise ticket definitely helped deflate whatever sense of accomplishment I had been feeling that night.

Later on, when I was finally able to look up my infraction on the speeding-ticket website, I found out I owed $170, exactly what I had made that night.

7

few days after my first night stripping, I had an interview at the Suburban Public Library. I had already gone on one public-library interview so far. The Ann Arbor District Library had called me for one of their shelving positions, which wouldn't do much for me in terms of professional experience but could at least help me get my foot in the door at a public library. Aurora already worked there as an information-desk clerk. However, I got mixed signals from the man who interviewed me. Knowing I was in library school, he indicated that he assumed I would want to move up from a shelving position since my application said I was in library school, and he didn't seem to approve of my obvious plan. He also seemed annoyed by the questions he was required to ask me; halfway through a question about what my greatest weakness was, he rolled his eyes and said he was skipping that one because it was stupid. The Suburban interview was higher-pressure, and the position was for a substitute library aide. The director explained that at their library, a "substitute" usually meant at least a shift or two per week.

Library aide was a generic term to describe someone who worked as support staff, and that meant different things at different libraries; it could mean working at the circulation desk or processing books in the back. In Suburban's case, library aides were basically public-service desk professionals. If I got the job, I would be getting reference-desk experience, which was exactly what I wanted.

At the end of the day, I still felt significantly less nervous about going to a library interview than doing an audition at a strip club. After that nerve-wracking experience, anything else seemed easy by comparison.

My main worry was that I was beginning to exude some type of inappropriate sexuality. As a stripper, I had to give off a level of sexuality I never expressed before in such a public way in front of so many people. I had opened a door that I was not sure I knew how to reclose and open completely on command. This was just the beginning of a long struggle with my double identity. I needed to come off as responsible and mature as possible in a library interview, but those were boring traits to give off when walking around a strip club.

On the day of the interview, I wore a blue polka-dot blouse, a black cardigan, and a grey pencil skirt with Mary Janes. I put my hair back in a ponytail, and the only makeup I wore was light foundation and a little mascara.

The interview went by very fast. I went into the building and asked for the director at the circulation desk. She came out and greeted me and then took me to the children's story-time room, which was set up with tables and small chairs for a craft event that she explained would be happening later that day.

I really can't remember the details of the questions she asked. I just know most of my answers reflected my interest in public library service and the types of classes I had taken thus far at SI. I made sure to smile and listen attentively. Plenty of people had told me that I wore a resting bitch face, so coming off as warm and friendly was going to be important in both the library and stripping worlds.

At the end of the interview, she was offering me the job. I didn't have to go home and wait to get a phone call—or worse, wait and not get one. I quickly accepted, and she went on to explain that my schedule would vary quite a bit from week to week, depending on when I was needed. If my second job had been waitressing, this irregularity would have been a big problem. But given that I could make my own schedule at Bogart's based on nights that were convenient for me, it would work out perfectly.

Before I started, the director said I would have to get a Michigan driver's license and then stop by City Hall to fill out some paperwork. The city of Suburban required me to be a Michigan resident to work for them. I had no problem doing it, but it felt a little weird after living in Illinois all my life. I still felt like a visitor in Michigan. Changing my license, however, would not in any way affect my out-of-state status at the University of Michigan. I had looked into that long before. A student enrolled as out of state would remain that way for the duration of her degree, regardless of any actions that established residency.

I didn't know what I had done right at that interview. Later, when I was trying to get a professional position as a librarian, I would go on to feel like I'd completely bombed interviews because I didn't get the job. It was quite possible that the director didn't want to have to go through a formal hiring process. She knew someone who could vouch for me, and so long as I didn't give off a bad impression at the interview, I could have the job.

I planned to get my license changed that next day, and the director picked a start date for me to come in and get trained on both the children's and adult reference desks. I was very excited. This would be the perfect experience and the one I needed to work professionally in public libraries.

My confidence about stripping shifted back and forth, over and over. On my second night at Bogart's, I still felt shy about going up and talking to people, so I started out sitting at the bar for about an hour. This time, I met a loquacious stripper named Angela who was complaining that she couldn't work at the club she usually worked at—Henry VIII's—because she had been caught smoking pot in the dressing room and they had suspended her for a month as a result.

"It's total BS because other girls there totally do it all the time. I was totally singled out because the manager doesn't like me."

"So you like working there more than here?" I was curious to learn about girls' experiences at other clubs. Henry VIII's, which was in the same town, didn't have that many reviews online, so I hadn't really considered it.

She leaned into me confidentially. "Oh, yeah. This place is so dirty. I keep seeing girls being straight-up nasty back there. The other night, I saw this girl with her hand down a customer's pants."

"Who was it?" I was being nosy. She was talking about one of the infamous "extras" girls I had heard about online.

Angela scanned the room. "I don't see her. But she knows who she is."

"No one does extras at Henry's? Maybe I should have tried that club instead."

"They don't put up with that shit there. You should check it out. I have to wait a few more weeks before I can go back."

Angela got called to the stage, and I continued to feel like an anxious weirdo about going up and talking to people.

Finally, a guy in a suit came up to me. "I just wanted to tell you that I was admiring you from across the room. You should have come over and said hi. I've got to go now, but maybe I'll see you next time."

I smiled stupidly and watched him walk out the door. Obviously, I was losing money with my passive approach. I resolved to start walking up to people and using the line I had decided on but had thus far failed to deliver.

I pinched myself and went up to a guy sitting alone. "Would you like some company?" That was the safest overture I could come up with and ended up being the way I usually started conversations with customers. It was a quick way to weed out customers who were not interested without having to experience too much rejection. If he said no, I would simply smile, tell the guy to enjoy his night, and move along.

I had two guys say no, but I wasn't surprised. I had already seen a few girls go up to them and not stay long. That was part of the job. On my third try, I got a yes from an elderly man who seemed like a sweet grandpa type.

After I sat down with the guy, he gave me a dollar bill and immediately began putting his hand on my leg. I tried making chitchat, asking him how his night was going and where he lived. He told me he lived nearby and came to the club sometimes. Then his hand began creeping up my leg. I brushed it away and asked him if that was his way of saying he wanted to get a dance. He went on to explain that he didn't get dances because he thought they were too expensive. Then he pulled out another dollar bill and tried to put his hand back on my leg closer to my crotch. I immediately stood up and told him I had to get going.

I found more guys to talk to but was not getting many dances. Finally, by eleven o'clock, DJ Russ called me up and asked for my house fee. I looked through my accumulated tips and realized I hadn't made it yet. He told me for future reference I had to pay by eleven every night and reminded me that it was only sixty dollars if I paid it before my shift started.

I walked away, embarrassed, and soon ended up on a side stage. I now had the incentive to work harder. I somehow got the drunk, enthusiastic guys sitting by my stage to tip me more and immediately brought the money up to DJ Russ. I wanted to get that over with. I would be paying up-front in the future.

I went back by the drunk guys and finally got one of them to get a dance with me. I got a few more dances that night but did not make out very well overall. I figured it was the second night and still a learning experience. The next time, I would try a weekend night—I finally felt ready for it.

It also became very clear that night that "Calliope" just wasn't working. I got way too many baffled expressions from guys when I told them my name. The next day, I discussed my name troubles with Aurora, and keeping with the Greek mythology theme, she suggested Penelope. I thought that was a good idea. It was recognizable and hopefully unique enough not to get me mixed up with another girl.

I found that getting to know some of the other girls at Bogart's made it easier to feel more comfortable navigating my new job as a stripper. I only saw my BFF Jenny one more time, so I did not know what happened to her. I also only saw Angela a few more times before bumping into her later at another club.

There were some girls who had seriously intimidating presences in the dressing room, but several others were friendly and helpful with my various dumb questions. Talking to the other girls was also a great way to recharge and fill the downtime when there weren't too many customers in the club.

The first regular girl I got to know was Gwen. She was a friendly Korean-American woman in her early thirties and a flight attendant as her day job. She told me that she didn't make enough money with the shifts she got and thought she could supplement with stripping. Gwen also said she thought it would be an interesting way to meet people. That was the kind of line I would have assumed someone would reserve for customers, but the more I saw Gwen in action, the more true it seemed. She described herself as not much of a hustler, which made me feel better because I was new to hustling myself. I usually saw her just sitting and chatting with customers at the bar. I didn't see her getting a lot of dances, and she didn't seem to make a lot of money.

I thought that maybe she had gotten into stripping because she was bored.

A playful Black girl with intense eyes, named India, befriended me one night to let me know how hot she thought my ass was. She point-blank gave me the advice that Black guys would like me because of it and that she wasn't worried about competing with me because they would be the kind of Black guys who liked white girls anyways. She kept pointing my ass out to the guys she talked to that night and kept making them tip me when I walked by. It was like having my own personal hype person for a night, and I think she was serious about hitting on me, but then I never saw her again at Bogart's.

I also met the real Jade, whose name I had not been able to use. She was a round-faced blond girl who had studied cosmetology and was stripping to take care of her young child. In my first few weeks, I was surprised how many men told me how natural my look was—as in, "Wow, you're not wearing that much makeup." I supposed that was a compliment, but it was weird because I was actually wearing a ton of makeup. I wore dark, thick cat-eye eyeliner, the kind of look I had honed in college for going out. I was sure my makeup was dramatic. Jade showed me, though, that the colors I was using for eye shadow were wrong in the lighting of the club, so I started using darker colors combined with light greens and turquoise.

I also developed a protectiveness over Jade. I had conversations with several customers, in which they would disparage her body and tell me she shouldn't be stripping. Clearly, there were plenty of men who liked her, though, because she made her money at the end of the day. I would usually say that everyone liked something different, and I'd quickly change the subject. For some guys, that was their stupid way of complimenting me, but I didn't want to hear it.

Another girl who stood out from my early days of stripping was a University of Michigan undergrad named Brooklyn, a short, thin, very tan brunette with pierced nipples. I had been hoping to meet other students who stripped. She told me she was majoring in biomechanical engineering, and I was impressed. She was only twenty, so she wasn't able to drink. Overall, my impression was that Brooklyn was very grounded and knew what she was doing. I appreciated watching her work because I knew she never played dumb with customers, which was a style I didn't think I could pull off, either. Like Angela, she'd had a good experience working at Henry VIII's.

When I would do something wrong, I was always corrected by another girl, never by management. I learned that certain poles onstage were just there for show and that I shouldn't be trying to swing around them. The metal poles were safe, and the plastic poles with the lights inside were not.

I also learned that I shouldn't attempt to hustle customers who were seated at the stage, only the guys at a table or the bar—unless one of them specifically invited me to sit down. It was considered rude to try to take their attention away from the girl onstage. A girl told me this matter-of-factly without being accusatory. I did not take these corrections personally. There were a lot of things I didn't know, and I had to find them out one way or another.

On one of the hourly finales, another girl scolded me for leaving my drink at a customer's table when I went to the stage. I had been planning on going back and thought leaving my drink was a good way to indicate that, but it wasn't very smart—any customer could try to take advantage of me by putting something in my drink. After that, any time I had a drink, I took it wherever I went in the club. That included not leaving it in the dressing room either.

I quickly stopped doing my makeup before work. I didn't like stopping on my way to pick up cigarettes or an energy drink and feeling self-conscious about how much makeup I had on. It was way too much in daylight, and I felt that it screamed that I was a stripper. I also stopped wearing the phony pony. I really liked the volume it gave my hair, but it would begin sinking the more I moved around, and I had to constantly readjust it. I started straightening my hair with a flatiron, and that seemed to work.

I wasted a lot of time and money trying different thongs. The ones I started with slid too easily, and I kept shifting back and forth between ones that were either too large or too small. I noticed many girls wore a lycra thong with a thick band that hung low on their hips, so I figured out how to get one of those. They were made specifically for stripping—thick enough to offer extra protection from grabby guys but small enough not to look like I was trying to hide something.

I discovered that one of my favorite nights to work was Tuesday. It was discount dance night, which meant we had to sell all dances for only ten dollars a song. At first, I thought that was too cheap to bother with, but then I realized how popular the night was and just how many more customers were there all night long. It was much easier to get dances and be busy than to waste a bunch of time trying to chat someone up and then have it lead nowhere.

I was still apprehensive of approaching tables with groups. I preferred talking to guys who were alone or in pairs. I would chat about the club or other clubs guys had been to, ask them what they did for fun, and try to keep things light. The name Penelope seemed to be going over better than Calliope, but customers continually wanted to know my real name. I was really surprised by that at first— it seemed like an obvious violation of the stripper-customer social contract. I would say things like, "But I'm not supposed to tell you that" in a playful way, but I could tell that offended them. That was annoying, but I realized these guys just wanted to feel as though I was being genuine with them. On some level, they knew that when they came into a strip club, they were there for a fantasy, but they didn't want it to feel like a fantasy. They wanted to feel as if they were more special than the last guy I gave dances to.

Not only was I bad at lying, but I just didn't feel comfortable doing it. Although several girls came up with completely made-up background stories for their stripper personas, everything I told customers was true until I started encountering questions that I considered too personal. So I started telling guys that my "real name" was Sara. No one questioned that one, and I continued with the same fake real name from customer to customer so I wouldn't forget it. And some customers would insist on calling me Sara once they thought that was my real name.

When I told people I lived in Ann Arbor and they started asking about neighborhoods and streets, I began making things up too. But I told them I was from Illinois and that I was a grad student at Michigan. If they pressed further, I would acknowledge I was studying to be a librarian. Theoretically, they could have looked me up online, but they would have only found one Sara enrolled in my program. I always wondered if she'd ever received a creepy email from some strange guy telling her he liked her lap dance.

I was surprised by how many guys would ask me out or try to make plans to see me outside of the club. Again, I thought this was an obvious violation of the strip club social contract: *What happens at the club stays at the club.* But as with knowing my real name, they wanted to feel like I was a real, accessible person and not just a fantasy they came into a strip club to see. All different types of customers asked me out. Some asked out every stripper they talked to, and others seemed more naively genuine about it.

The first guy who asked me out was a University of Michigan hockey player who had never been to a strip club before. I fumbled my answer to him because I was so surprised. I looked at him, confused, and told him he wasn't supposed to ask me that. Then he started apologizing and became embarrassed. I wished I had handled that more gracefully.

I started just telling guys that I didn't date customers, period, and they could always come see me in the club. It was nothing personal, but I had to separate my lives inside the club and outside. Most guys understood, but some still acted offended.

I also had to find a creative way to handle guys who wanted my phone number, which was another way many of them tried to arrange contacting girls outside of the club. Some girls gave guys their numbers without any fear and then used them to bring their regulars in to come see them on slow nights. I was definitely not comfortable with that kind of arrangement and quickly learned to pretend my cell phone wasn't even with me so a customer would be free to leave his number on a napkin or give me a business card if he really wanted to. I had made the mistake of agreeing to program a guy's number into my phone, and then he requested proof that I had actually programmed it in by calling him. Without thinking, I hit the call button and immediately regretted it. He knew from the look on my face that I'd never intended for him to have my number, and then I was stuck being afraid he might actually call me at some point just to mess with me. Luckily, that never happened.

There were rules against guys having their cell phones out, because they weren't allowed to take pictures. At the time, most camera phones wouldn't have taken very good pictures in the dark club anyways, but they made me nervous nonetheless. I imagine that the phone situation in clubs is even harder to avoid now with significantly better camera-phone resolution, people texting all the time, and most having data phones. It would be so easy for a guy to snap a picture and immediately upload it to social media before a bouncer could intervene and make him delete it from his phone.

One of my first memorable customers was an architect When I approached him to ask him if he would like some company, he hesitated for a moment, a bit sullenly, but then said yes. When he told me he usually liked blondes, I thought things were going to go south and I should probably just move along. Then I told him my name was Penelope, and he lit up. The architect explained that he was Italian and liked my name as an homage to the classics. We ended up talking a long time about a variety of topics, including Dostoevsky and *Six Feet Under*, while I gave him ten lap dances. At the end of the night, he asked me out, and I had to explain my rule. Thereafter, I always thought back to him as a sort of ideal customer: well-behaved, buying lots of dances, and easy to have a conversation with.

His business card ended up in my growing collection. I was beginning to consider creating a collage out of all the unsolicited contact info I had accumulated from customers.

8

My schedule at the Suburban library was variable. Most weeks, I had at least two shifts that lasted five to six hours, and they were often on the weekends. Most of the time, I didn't start till noon, so I could work at Bogart's the night before I worked at Suburban, or even go in at night after a library shift.

As a library aide, I spent about half my time at the reference desk. Suburban had an even mix of librarians and library aides. I had the same desk responsibilities as the librarians except that I didn't have enough regular hours to be in charge of an area of the collection or do library programming, which are all the book clubs, story times, and other events libraries put together for the public.

That semester, I was also taking a class on reference resources, which most people at SI took their first year. Even in 2005, however, I did not end up using a lot of actual print resources with my patrons.

Public library patrons did not often have highly research-intensive questions. Many common questions just involved finding street directions and searching for symptoms on WebMD. At that point, SI was still holding out that the best way to find anything online was to use multiple search engines, but everyone I knew found that in actual practice, Google gave the best results. Of course, we were proven right in the long run.

We also introduced people to databases, an underutilized resource available through most libraries. It was often difficult to explain to people the difference between information anyone could access online and information available through subscription database services. I would often have to reassure high school students that information I helped them find through a database was not considered an Internet resource, because many teachers would restrict how many Internet sources they were allowed to use for their papers.

Another inevitable part of working any public library reference desk was helping patrons use computers. We did not have very many computers, so there was often a waitlist, which at first we handled with paper. We'd have to go up to people after their thirty minutes were over and ask them to get off for the next person. That request did not always go over well, although everyone was told before they got on how much time they were allotted.

Many people who came in did not have computer skills, and I often ended up standing over them, doing things like setting up their first email account or formatting a word document. At first, my philosophy was to just to do whatever the patron asked from us as far as using a computer went, whether it made sense or not. I didn't feel it was right to factor my opinion into the matter when someone was just trying to go about their business, even if I couldn't make sense of what they were doing.

Eventually, I began to see that it was sometimes appropriate to give suggestions, such as when someone was trying to make a professional document. I would point out spell-check and try to explain why someone would want to use that feature. One early incident that stood out was a young woman making her first résumé because a job she was interested in applying for had told her she had to have one. I gave her a template to start filling out, and when she came to get me because she had a question, I saw that she had entered "none" under suggested fields such as "Volunteer Work" and

"Professional Associations." I realized that my role should include suggesting to her that she should completely delete those categories instead of leaving them there to highlight experience she did not have.

One of the most fun types of questions librarians were asked at the reference desk were readers' advisory requests. People commonly wanted suggestions for books to read based on favorite authors or other books they'd enjoyed. To help with the wide variety of questions I encountered, I had to learn about genre fiction I hadn't read. People wanted help finding Amish fiction, Westerns, sailing stories, cozy mysteries with no sex or swearing, and read-a-likes for authors I had no familiarity with. I used Amazon's recommendation system, which was still fairly new at the time, and a database called Novelist. Eventually, I was more familiar with all the diverse genres of fiction people were interested in.

The other half of my time at the library was spent at the children's desk. There I assisted children of different ages and their parents in finding books. Children, however, could be vague about exactly what they wanted. Often kids would ask for a good chapter book, and I'd ask them a bunch of questions about what they'd read before and enjoyed. Did they like mysteries? Did they like books that took place in the past? And of course, did they like magic, wizards, and dragons? One time, a nine-year-old girl asked me, "Do you have any books where it starts really interesting and then gets even more interesting?" And really, who doesn't want a book like that?

The Children's Department was usually slower than the reference desk. In the downtime, I would ask my coworkers if they needed any help, but the answer was usually no, so I would explore the picture books I used to read as a child. It was a fun sort of nostalgia, but I soon realized it would be helpful to learn about all the new kids' books that had come out in the last twenty years as well.

My coworkers at Suburban knew I had another job, which I had at first just vaguely described as waitressing. But naturally, the question of where I was waitressing came up in conversation. I had been somewhat prepared for that and had discussed it ahead of time with Aurora. As usual, I relied on her to help me craft the nomenclature of my secret identity. I told them I was working at a bar called Archie's. The bar did not exist. I couldn't use a real restaurant because it was possible one of them would consider visiting on a night when I said I was working. It would be easy enough for any of them to do a Google search to find out more about Archie's and find absolutely nothing, which of course would be suspicious as well.

Now I was lying in my "real" life, and it felt weird. Most of my life, I had probably been too honest with people, so that new approach made me feel anxious.

Meanwhile, I was working three to four nights a week at Bogart's. I still hadn't actually spoken with the manager. I saw him talk to other girls here or there but only because they went up to him to initiate a conversation. He really just looked like any other guy at a bar, drinking his pain away and staring at sports on TV. The one benefit in knowing he was the manager was that I avoided the embarrassment of going up to him to hustle dances.

DJ Russ seemed to be the one handling the logistics, taking house fees, planning who danced when, and letting girls know anything new—he was much happier announcing Penelope as my stage name. There wasn't really anyone bossing us. Theoretically, the bouncers were supposed to stop too much from going on in the private dance room, but I never saw that happen.

I only saw the house mom shout "Hey!" once, when two girls started getting on each other about a customer in the dressing room. That stopped the tiff right there. I had heard stories about a recent bad dressing room fight that involved a stiletto, and it was hard to imagine what the mom had done when it happened.

I did talk to our house mom more and got a better understanding of her lethargy. She was seriously tired. Apparently, she worked every shift, day and night, that the club was open, just sitting there on her stool. That meant she was there from eleven in the morning till two a.m. every night Monday through Saturday and then from two in the afternoon till closing on Sunday, so she essentially only got one day a week to sleep in. She also only made the money that we tipped out to her, which meant the club was treating her as an independent contractor as well. I found that out one night when she was tipsy and gushing about how much fun she'd had at the casino the Saturday night before. It had been her one time to get out and have some fun, at three in the morning.

This lady had definitely lived a hard life. A customer told me about how the house mom had ventured out of the dressing room once and wandered drunkenly onto the stage to dance for the customers. He explained it as an unpleasant experience. Of course, she'd once been a stripper herself. Most house moms started out that way. But I had to imagine that for her it had been many years before.

I discovered that my boundaries were a lot more lenient than I thought they were going to be in terms of mileage during a lap dance, but they were still pretty conservative compared to some of the girls I observed in the dance room. The girl who gave the most extras was Margo. She arrived every night a few hours late, which meant she had to pay ten dollars an hour more in house fees and then had less time to make her money. That apparently was not an issue for Margo, though. She got lap dance after lap dance and seemed to be able to pull guys into the back room without investing more than two minutes talking to them. Although I never heard anything she said to them out on the floor, it was easy to infer the type of things she was offering. In the back room, Margo made out with most of her customers, let them put their hands down her thong, and gave hand jobs. It was unclear whether she even charged extra for those services or just offered them as part of a standard dance. Either way, she was the busiest girl on any given night.

Margo wasn't the only girl who did those kinds of "dances," but she was by far the most flagrant. Other girls at least made some effort to conceal what they were doing. As a stripper, I had no problem with higher contact sex work, but it was hard to compete with that as an easy alternative in the same club where I was trying to sell lap dances. I began to consider trying another club. I was tired of how many guys were pushing for more during a lap dance. Some nights were fine, but others, every other guy either didn't want to get dances with me because I wouldn't make out with him, or only got a dance or two because I wasn't taking it further.

I was still too intimidated to try one of the fancier gentlemen's clubs, and since two girls had already recommended Henry VIII's, it seemed like the logical next club to try. Henry's was only about another mile down the road.

Of course, the day I decided to give Henry's a try, I was extremely nervous again. I wasn't so worried about getting hired this time but was more nervous about navigating a completely new club and dealing with all new people. As I expected, there wasn't really an audition—Henry VIII's and Bogart's were owned by the same guy. I just had to talk to the manager, who told me to put my name on the list and asked for a house fee, for which I was prepared to pay up front this time. His name was Fred and he seemed like a pretty nonexpressive type of person, which didn't surprise me at all by that point.

My first night there ended up being pretty lucrative. I was better prepared to take advantage of customers' interest in the new girl than I had been on my first night at Bogart's. I found a customer who wanted several dances right after the first showcase of evening girls. Although the club wasn't very busy most of the night, I still did well without having to work too hard or avoid getting mauled.

Henry's, though, was dumpier than Bogart's. The main stage was more of a platform, and the building was oddly shaped, so not everyone could see the main stage from where they were sitting. The dressing room was incredibly tiny, but there was a completely separate women's bathroom, so girls could distribute themselves between the two for more space. The private dance room was pretty dark but better removed from the rest of the club so everyone couldn't see the top of your head when you were giving a dance. The whole club was actually darker, with black lights instead of the red lights Bogart's had. Overall, I liked the lighting better than at Bogart's and thought it was more flattering for my complexion.

The DJ came up and introduced herself—I was surprised to discover she was a woman. I found it refreshing. She was a short lesbian, built like a little sprite, in her early forties and with an unfortunate feathered hairdo. Her name was Jean, and she was probably the only person working there who was friendly to me that night.

I kept my head down and tried to stay out of the other girls' way while still giving off a friendly vibe. No girls talked to me, which was fine. They were used to girls who just came in and worked one night, and there was usually no point in getting to know someone unless they kept coming back. One girl, however, did try to make me feel uncomfortable. She was a thick Amazon with long red hair, and she made a point of announcing that it smelled like cat piss every time I was in the dressing room with her. I later learned her name was Autumn.

If that had happened on my very first night stripping, I might have felt too intimidated to come back. But by the time I started at Henry's, I knew it was something that happened sometimes, especially with new girls, and I wasn't afraid to go back and work around Autumn again. I would just continue to keep my head down and not give her a reason to dislike me. Looking back on it later, I realized she only tried to intimidate me because I had done well that night.

9

---●○●---

I quickly learned that the signup sheet at Henry's was left on a ledge outside the dressing room for anyone, including customers, to walk by and see. When you came in each night, you were supposed to sign in with your stage name and then your real name in the second column. My signature was already pretty scribbly, but I went ahead and turned it into utter gibberish with a big S at the front to represent my "Sara" identity. I even had a customer comment that I had an illegible signature, which just proved that they sometimes stopped to look at the clipboard if they noticed it on the way to the bathroom. I was surprised I was the only person paranoid about that being out there.

The girls at Henry's were a little tougher to crack than the girls at Bogart's. I remained as unobtrusive as possible and tried to stay out of everyone's way, especially in the dressing room.

One of the first women to be friendly to me was an older lady named Heaven. She had been working at Henry's for many years and often worked double shifts, which meant she got there before noon when the club opened and stayed until two in the morning. She needed to work that much longer because she got fewer dances than the other women. She had breast implants, and I thought she was good-looking for her age—forty-four—but her front teeth were messed up due to her ex-husband hurting her.

Heaven was a sweet lady, but I would soon learn she had a reputation for being kind of crazy. I got the sense that she talked about the most random things with customers and gave what she considered more traditional lap dances rather than the typical hard grind a lot of guys expected. She often talked about her teenage son, who was on the spectrum, and how she worried about him and hoped he could go to college. She liked me because she thought I was smart, and she kept asking my advice about things he should be doing to get ready for college.

I managed to stay off Autumn's radar after the first night. It probably helped that I had not done as well on my next few nights. The roster the bouncers kept in the private dance room recorded how many dances we did, so a girl could go by and check how well she was doing compared to everyone else.

I also learned that Autumn had other girls to take her meanness out on. One night, she was bitching about a girl named Gloria she had seen letting a guy finger her in the back room. "I swear to God, if I see that shit again, I'm going to fuck that bitch up!" I clearly wasn't as high on her people-to-bully scale as I initially imagined.

I realized that Autumn's attitude, and that of the other regular girls with strong personalities, was probably what kept Henry's from getting as high mileage as some of the other clubs. If extras were going on, Autumn would sniff them out and make sure the offender got really uncomfortable with continuing to work there.

On the other hand, Gloria was one of the first girls to be nice to me. I wondered why she and some of the other girls always used the bathroom as their dressing room and only dashed into the actual dressing room to secure their stuff in a locker. At first, I thought they wanted to use the extra counter space in the bathroom, but then I realized they were usually avoiding Autumn and another outspoken girl named Rose.

Rose had a way of taking up a lot of space, while still not being that big herself, and she would very directly let you know if you were where she wanted to be. She was a small athletic Afro-Latina woman with a beautiful mane of long black curly hair. I later found out that although she usually worked at least three to four nights a week, she drove even farther than me to work at Henry's because she also wanted to keep her stripping job and civilian life in Ohio completely separate. Although she had worked at Henry's for seven years, her friends and family believed she was working at a restaurant in Michigan.

Gloria had long blond hair and a very pretty face. She often wore outfits that covered her stomach, such as little dresses that she could pull down to just below her breasts onstage. She was really self-conscious of her stomach, she explained to me, because of stretch marks. Like many other girls I met, she was stripping to support her two small children.

I wanted to give Gloria the benefit of the doubt about doing extras because I was not convinced that Autumn was credible. I decided to only believe someone was doing extras if I saw it myself. Plus, at the end of the day, there was really no point in worrying too much about what everyone else was doing, especially if there was not much I could do about it.

A lot of the girls I worked with were mothers. Dawn had just had a baby a few months before. She explained, "My man sent me back to work, and he stays home with the baby. I was hoping I could stop stripping after I had him, but my man just can't get a job that pays what he's worth right now. So he says I have to keep stripping for now." She said this as though it were completely normal for her boyfriend to have that kind of authority over her.

One time, I found Dawn crying in the dressing room on the phone with her boyfriend. She just kept saying, "I'm sorry, I'll try harder. I'm sorry, I'll try harder." When she got off the phone, she explained, "My man has me call him to check in and tell him how I'm doing. And I haven't made very much yet tonight."

"Wait. So he's mad at you for not making enough?" I had to make sure I was hearing this correctly.

"Yeah."

"Couldn't you just not tell him or not answer the phone or something?" Or ditch his pathetic ass, I thought.

"He always knows," she said. "He always counts everything when I get home, anyways."

"So basically he thinks he's your pimp?" I asked carefully.

"Yeah, but he helps keep me motivated to hustle."

Fuck. She was defending him. Dawn's shitty situation was the first stereotypical stripper relationship I'd run into but unfortunately not the last. From my perspective, a person had to be pretty tough to handle being a stripper. Or at least, I felt as though I had to pull from some reserve of resilience to deal with all the bullshit many customers tried to do. I had observed Dawn in action, and she seemed like a good hustler. I thought that some of those skills would have translated into helping her not put up with such crap in her personal life.

Two of the highest earners were girls who usually liked to hustle together: Megan and Cherry. They were good at approaching groups of guys and getting lots of dances out of them. I first met Cherry making chitchat in the dressing room. We both liked to arrive early so we had plenty of time to get ready. She was a little thick and had an impressive confidence in talking to customers. I think she was more willing to be friendly to me than some of the other high-earning regular girls because she was still a newer dancer herself. She had been working there for less than a year. Cherry had previously had a decent job working as an administrative assistant at a community college, but when she lost her job, she needed to find a way to support her two children while her fiancé finished up his law degree.

Megan had a sugar daddy who had been taking care of her for a few months. She came back to work after I had already started and was very cold to me from the get-go. She didn't seem to like Cherry talking to me. Megan used to have a stage name but decided to start using her real name "because everyone knew it anyways." She was proud of that decision, because it came off as more genuine to customers. I learned that Megan had worked at Henry's since she was eighteen, and it was the only job she had ever had. By the time I met her, she was twenty-three and had three children.

Most of the other women I met weren't nearly as interested in anonymity as I was. A lot of them were open about being strippers to most of the people in their lives except for their children. Cherry and Megan gave their phone numbers out to customers all the time. I often saw them calling customers in the dressing room, trying to encourage them to come in that night and get some dances.

I was beginning to see that keeping some type of contact with customers helped improve business. I tried to work fairly regular days so when guys said they wanted to see me again, I could tell them when to come in. But that approach didn't always work, because sometimes I had to change my schedule because of schoolwork or my job at Suburban.

One of the other regular high earners who fascinated me was Porsche. She was totally gorgeous and only seemed to need to work about two nights a week. She had a few very dedicated regulars who came in to see her all the time. I never ever saw her hustle—she didn't need to. She already had the customer base, so she didn't have to deal with walking up to new people and making conversation. I could tell she was an introvert, like me, but she had the advantage of her beauty and had spent years cultivating regulars back when hustling was supposedly easier—which I kept hearing all the veteran girls tell me.

One time, I was talking to two guys, and one of them wanted to get dances with me, but first I had to find someone for his friend.

Porsche was actually alone at that moment, and his friend was pointing her out to me. I told him I'd go bring her over, but when I went to talk to her and tell her there was a guy interested in getting some dances with her, she looked at me as if I had two heads. I always welcomed easy business like that, when someone just handed me a customer, so I was surprised by her reaction. After Porsche wiped the confused expression off her face, she did come along and give the friend dances. I figured she just wasn't used to someone else working with her, since she didn't talk to the other girls very much.

Like Bogart's, the management at Henry's was pretty hands-off. The two night managers at least knew who I was, though, and sometimes even gave me a nod of recognition when I came in for my shift. The only time I was ever criticized was on a slow night when there were almost no guys in club. I took a book out and sat down to read it at the bar. I would have read it in the dressing room, but I thought I should at least be somewhat aware if any new guys came in. I protested that there was no one in the bar to even care but still got a headshake from Fred. I wanted to point out that some guy might find my reading sexy, but I didn't think he would care. I probably could have gotten away with reading in another corner of the bar where Fred wouldn't have noticed me, but everywhere else was too poorly lit.

I continued to drink steadily through most nights, so I was at least tipsy until midnight, when I would switch to energy drinks. I needed alcohol for the social lubrication, but it also helped me to stay enthusiastic onstage, which was hard with most of the music selection. I got used to dancing to mediocre bands like Nickleback, Kid Rock, Linkin Park, 3 Doors Down, Switchfoot, and Lifehouse. Generic rock music was apparently the number-one preference for strip club customers. I also got to dance to gems like "Save a Horse [Ride a Cowboy]" by Big & Rich and "I'm in Love with a Stripper" by T-Pain, featuring Mike Jones. Each night ended with Semisonic's "Closing Time," which at first I found annoying and repetitive. But anyone who works in a bar can begin to appreciate the song when they finally hear the line, "You don't have to go home, but you can't stay here."

10

I was adjusting to my double life and learning to make the necessary transitions from student to librarian to stripper and back again, but it was still stressful. As I was learning to operate out of my comfort zone in the strip club, I was getting more withdrawn in my regular life. This time, it was more out of a sense of avoidance than depression. I had little interest in a social life, because that would mean meeting new people and having to negotiate how much I disclosed. For that reason, dating felt off the table, but I had pretty much decided that when I started stripping anyway.

The oddest days for me were when I worked at both Suburban and Henry's. My weekend shifts—Friday, Saturday, or Sunday—were usually twelve to five at Suburban, so it often made sense to just go into Henry's at seven. I would stop somewhere to get something to eat and read a book to kill a little time. That was when I was in the strangest, most anxious state of mind—sitting somewhere in public, trying to mentally transition from acting serious and responsible to being sexy and fun.

Sometimes I stopped at a tanning salon by the library, and I always worried that it was suspicious that someone who worked in a library tanned. Looking back, I'm not really sure how that would've stood out in any way. People usually tan because they like having tan skin, not because they're strippers. The paranoia about getting found out was real for me. One day, a guy recognized me at a nearby gas station and said hi. I couldn't identify how I knew him, so I thought he was a customer, and I almost had a panic attack until he told me I came into his tanning salon.

When I drove to Henry's from home, the longer car trip in rush hour traffic gave me the time I needed to mentally shift over. When I arrived, I had my plain street clothes on and my hair in a sloppy ponytail and was wearing glasses. I would walk through the club and rush straight to the dressing room. Every now and then, a customer would try to stop me to talk, but I would smile and wave him off. I needed my locker room ritual in order to be ready to interact with customers as Penelope.

I usually got there at least forty-five minutes before my shift. I liked having plenty of time to straighten my hair, put my contacts in, and do my makeup. I was also still wearing the elaborate patent leather bondage boots that took some time to get tied and fastened. If I was in a rush, it would make getting ready more stressful.

Whenever I planned to work on a Saturday, I had to take into account the Michigan football schedule. I lived near the Big House, and my landlord's nephews would come over and let people pay them to park in my apartment's parking lot during home games, boxing in all of the residents so we couldn't leave. Although I'd lived there for two years, I still never really got used to how intense the tailgating could get in my neighborhood.

One day when that happened, I gave in and decided to just walk to campus to get some schoolwork done at the library and work the next night instead. I walked past probably one hundred tailgating parties and got yelled at by three different groups of drunken guys because I was not wearing maize and blue (the colors of The University of Michigan). With my headphones in my ears and book bag on my back, I was obviously going to go study. One guy actually followed me half a block to offer me a beer and tell me how lame I was for being such a party pooper. Situations like that always gave me a stupid urge to say something like, "I'm a stripper. I know how to party. I just don't want to come to your stupid football party." But of course, that would have opened up a whole conversation I didn't really want to have. On home-game days, I would leave early and go camp out at a coffee shop somewhere far from campus until I could go into work.

I realized my nights started more efficiently if I had alcohol in my system earlier rather than later. Otherwise, I might waste too much time starting the night reluctant to talk to people because no one had bought me a drink yet. I could have bought myself a drink, but most drinks—including a bottle of swill beer—started at seven dollars. I wanted to preserve my money, so I often stopped at the liquor store and bought a half pint of Jägermeister to keep in a brown bag in my locker. I was well aware that this was not a healthy thing to be doing, but I still considered this part of my life something that I could compartmentalize and work to improve upon later.

Somehow, this approach was helping me control my drinking when I didn't work. I realized that I was rarely drinking on the nights that I stayed in, and it was unusual for me to go out. I still spent my free nights lying in bed, doing homework, and then getting immersed in a TV on DVD marathon.

My covert Jäger bottles were what finally helped endear me to my more resistant coworkers. When I had a getting-to-know-you conversation with any of the girls in the dressing room and it came out that I was working on a master's degree at Michigan, I often got a weird silence as if they just didn't know what to make of that information. They were probably trying to decide if I was really one of them. Attending graduate school at an elite university represented a class divide, but at the same time, I was there working the pole with them.

I knew that working-class people encountered plenty of people with degrees who had put them down for not having the same life advantages. It was reasonable for them to be wary that I might be that way as well.

My paper-bag liquor turned out to be the perfect bridge. I would just take a few swigs from my paper bag as I got ready. At first, no one noticed because I was trying to be subtle. There was always the possibility that one of the girls would tell the manager and I would get in trouble—although I suspected the worst punishment I would receive would be to have my Jäger confiscated.

It was Rose, who was just as intimidating as Autumn, who first noticed. "Whoa, girl. What are you drinking there?"

I pulled out my bottle to show her.

"Oh, girl, you're going to get in trouble if they see that. Make sure you don't do that in front of Heaven. That crazy bitch is all up in Curly's shit." She stuck her hand out, and I gave her the bottle so she could take a drink.

Autumn came into the dressing room at that point.

"Look at Penelope hiding her little paper bag of Jäger," Rose said, and they both snickered. There was something funny about me drinking before work, but more than that, it made me more accessible. Despite being a stripper, I had been giving off the impression that I was sheltered or proper in some way that didn't quite make sense. Being caught with a paper bag of Jäger gave them a taste of my weaknesses, which somehow made everything else I did thereafter seem cute and eccentric to Rose and Autumn.

"You know, you should put that in a plastic coke bottle. No one would suspect that," Autumn suggested after she stopped laughing.

"That's a good idea."

I followed Autumn's advice and ended up a lot less worried about getting caught.

* * *

When I considered the time I put into stripping, I had to add all the extra boring body-maintenance tasks I was doing as well. If I wasn't dating anyone, I normally got lazy about shaving in the colder months, but once I started stripping, I had to do it religiously. I was very prone to razor burn, so I had to time my shaving carefully and perform an elaborate moisturizing ritual to decrease my tendency to get the dreaded red bumps. I had to be vigilant about hair removal because I couldn't have anything hanging out of my G-string.

A few days a week, I would wear a bright green facial mask for twenty minutes, which tightened my pores. I had to combat all the oil I was putting on my face with constant makeup. When I got home from work, I had to scrub my face down or I would regret it the next day when I woke up with scary raccoon eyes.

I thought I might have to keep up a diet-and-exercise routine to keep my figure, but the stage time at Henry's burned off whatever I was eating and drinking. I also didn't eat a lot on days I worked, because the food made me more tired, which made it harder to keep going until two in the morning. I would usually only eat a Cliff Bar before my shift, and when I got home, I'd have a big noodle soup.

I kept planning to go to the tanning salon at least three times a week, but I usually ended up only doing it about once a week because standing still in a UV coffin was hard when I was so jittery. I was paler than most of the other girls, but the minimal tan base I was maintaining kept me from looking green in the black lights of the club.

Compared to my usual skin tone, though, I was very tan. I got unreasonably paranoid that people at school would find it suspicious that I was tanner than I'd been the previous year, especially as the year moved into winter. I was always afraid I would unintentionally do something strippery, like laugh a little too dramatically at someone's joke and then accidentally make inappropriate come-hither eyes, because I'd forgotten to turn Penelope off. To overcompensate, I grew more reserved in outside social situations.

I was also nervous when I went to the bank to deposit my stacks of cash. I was surprised by how many bank tellers had no discretion in speculating aloud how I had come by that much cash. I would have thought not discussing the who, what, and why of people's money was part of their training. When I was a waitress, I had gotten the same types of comments as a joke: "Oh, how did you get so many singles?" Wink. Wink. At the time, it hadn't mattered because I didn't have anything to hide.

When I got a nosy teller, I learned to nip that kind of conjecture in the bud by saying that I was a waitress who had simply not gone to the bank in a long time. The tellers were probably just trying to make conversation. Recounting my cash for deposit took longer than most other transactions, and as a result, I stood in front of them for a while. Many service workers felt obligated to make conversation when they were dealing with someone for an extended period of time. I just wanted them to move off the topic of the origin of my money. That kind of joking made me anxious because I was already overly paranoid.

My roommate, Aurora, was the only person around me who knew what I was doing at first. It was great to have her there to talk to about my experiences. She was always supportive and amused by my stories.

Aurora and I also talked a lot about the different assignments we had in our programs. She was much more satisfied with her coursework at Wayne State than she had been at Michigan. It was more hands-on and practical for actually working in a library. She had more assignments that related specifically to the types of policies libraries had to draft and defend, as well as dealing with ways to organize programming for patrons. The only two classes at SI that specifically addressed what someone needed to know when working in a public library were the reference materials class I was taking and the collection development class I was signed up to take in my last semester.

Like me, Aurora did not get out much. She spent a lot of time in her room, Skyping with a guy from the UK she had met online. They had a whirlwind romance and had gotten engaged before ever actually meeting in person.

I was nervous for her when he came for his first visit. I wondered whether things would dissolve when they met in real life. It seemed to me that pheromones were an important part of attraction. I was happy to work the first night they met so that they were alone together in the apartment. They were asleep—or at least sounded asleep—by the time I got home.

When I saw Aurora the next day, I was able to get the look from her that told me everything had gone well. Her beau, Brian, stayed quietly in her room while I got ready to go to campus, and I came back to the apartment in the afternoon still having not met him.

When Brian finally emerged from Aurora's room, he did not look at me when I tried to say hi to him. I'd never been an aggressive greeter, so I did not pursue talking to him when he went to the fridge and grabbed a soda to take back to Aurora's room.

My first reaction was to get pissed and begin overdramatizing the situation in my mind. The way I saw it, a strange man was staying in my apartment, and he didn't see any reason to make me feel comfortable with his presence by being friendly. I grabbed my keys, got into the car, and began calling friends to complain. I couldn't get a hold of anyone, and as I drove around, I began to calm down and realize I was overreacting. Brian was probably just nervous and shy. I shouldn't take it as an offense, because it wasn't about me.

I decided to go back to the apartment and try harder to be friendly. I realized I was learning to react more maturely and not turn ordinary situations into dramas, which I had done way too much as an undergrad. I also recognized that I had been more successfully executing this mature approach in more and more areas of my life. Avoiding drama was, after all, a prerequisite to surviving at a strip club.

When I got back, Aurora had come home from work, and she invited me to go out to dinner with them. Everything ended up going fine with Brian.

11

I learned a lot in my first few months of stripping.

Reactions from customers implied that there was something funny about my answer to the question "Where do you live?" Finally, I asked a guy about it and learned that saying you were from Ann Arbor sometimes gave people the perception that you were a snob. Apparently, many people in Southeastern Michigan saw Ann Arbor as a rich, liberal place that thought it was smarter and better than everyone else. I was still relatively new to Michigan, but over time, I saw that they weren't wrong.

My hustling style varied a lot on any given night. When I was confident and the night was going well, it was easier to keep talking to people and getting dances. When the night was bad, it was hard to maintain the momentum to keep going, and I felt less adept at small talk and persuading men to get dances with me.

I had always been passive about seducing people in my own intimate relationships. I wasn't the initiator with men, although I was more likely to initiate with women. As a stripper, I too often waited for the customer to suggest getting a dance. Consequently, I would sometimes waste too much time making chitchat. I avoided getting too overtly sexual in conversations and tended to steer things away from going too far in that direction because I didn't want to deal with the inevitable expectations. I ended up doing best with guys who either liked talking to me or came in without much desire to chat and just found me to be their "type"—whatever that meant.

My look was dark but not quite goth. Although I had the long black hair, I wore bright-teal sparkly eye makeup with cat-eye eyeliner, red lipstick, big glittering earrings, and a fake-gemstone choker. I was somewhere on the pinup-to-glam-to-fetish spectrum, if such a thing existed. I had a few vinyl tops, but then, I also wore tiny dresses that were reminiscent of revealing 1950s bathing suits. One of my simpler outfits, which I wore often, was a small black triangle bra with a tiny camouflage pleated skirt that went nicely with my big patent leather boots.

Going into stripping, I had a good sense of what my stronger features were, but I learned even more from the unsolicited comments of guys. I would never actually ask anyone, "What do you think about the way I look?" I knew I had a little bit of a paunch that was never completely flat, even at my thinnest. Drinking beer every night I worked probably didn't help that. I also thought my arms were kind of thick, but I got compliments from customers on my "athletic" build. Basically, I grew muscle easily, and twirling around the pole was helping keep up my triceps definition.

My big butt was popular with ass enthusiasts. It had a nice round shape, and I had the good fortune to not have accumulated any stretch marks at that point in my life. A few guys even accused me of having butt implants, which sounded like the most uncomfortable thing ever. I also got compliments on how white and straight my teeth were. I realized they were that way because of the privilege of having had access to orthodontic work as a child, which many of the women I worked with did not have.

Interestingly, I also got compliments on my lack of tattoos. Many guys told me I looked as if I should have some, and then they would congratulate me on not having any. I had never consciously decided to not get a tattoo and had thought about it plenty of times, but I always figured if I got one, it should be something I really wanted for a long time. On the other hand, there were also guys who were really into tattoos, and they would encourage me to get some ink. I was getting plenty of advice about my body all the time, which many guys felt welcome to give when it was on display.

Probably the weirdest unsolicited recommendation came from men who told me not to get breast implants. They would always say this in such an earnest way. Not all men liked large breasts, but it was funny how many of them felt I needed to be warned away from enlarging mine. I never asked them what they thought about my small boobs or indicated in any way that I was worried about their size.

Customers told me I looked like Michelle Williams, Jennifer Tilley, and Fran Drescher. I was taken aback by the latter, which I actually heard twice. The guys assured me that they meant that as a compliment and they thought Fran Drescher was good-looking. I, however, felt self-conscious and worried that there was something grating about my voice that was eliciting the mental image of her character in *The Nanny*.

I could tell by the way a guy said "no" that he just wasn't interested in me. Some guys didn't go for my look—they preferred bigger boobs or blond hair or whatever else. Some of the more aggressive hustlers I worked with could break past the barrier with reluctant guys because they didn't mind hearing "no" multiple times, so they tried harder. To them, it was worth the effort if it led to more dances, because some of those guys could still be convinced to say yes.

Some of the more aggressive hustling techniques I saw included things like straight-up crotch grabs. Autumn used that approach, and it worked well for her a lot of the time. A lot of guys came in to get as much physical contact with strange women as possible, but the crotch grab seemed like a form of sexual assault to me. There had to be some guys who were uncomfortable with a girl doing that to their bodies despite the kind of environment we were operating in.

There was also a fifty-year-old dancer named Nancy who didn't hide her age and the fact that she was a grandmother. She would pull on a guy's arm in the direction of the private dance room. That method encountered plenty of resistance, and I learned it was sometimes beneficial to sweep over to the table she had just been at, approach the guy who'd just gotten his arm pulled, and attempt to charm him with my lack of aggression.

Although I could see some of the physical techniques girls used successfully, I was still curious about what some of the other hustlers were saying to get dances. It was too loud to hear others in the club, though, and "What do you say to customers to get dances?" would have been an awkward question to bring up in the dressing room. If a girl had a strategy that was working for her, she probably didn't want to share what it was, because it might affect her income if other people started adopting that technique too.

In addition to the dance statistics that the bouncer in front of the private dance room kept, many girls would compare their earnings at the end of the night. Often, the amounts that some of the higher earners reported aloud didn't really match the number of dances the bouncer had recorded for them throughout the night. People must have exaggerated what they made sometimes. All the stripper support advice I read online said never to talk about your earnings with the other girls in the club, but it was hard to follow that when girls would regularly ask me how I made out at the end of the night. I usually claimed about fifty dollars more than I actually made, and as I got better and began making more money, I was careful to report below some of the more alpha personalities like Autumn and Megan, so I wouldn't be seen as a threat.

As I got more experienced, I learned more about how to fulfill my fantasy role while still seeming accessible to my customers. I had gotten tired of the number of guys who were asking me out, though. Some girls could keep the con going that they would eventually go out with customers who kept pursuing them, but for me, it wasn't worth the grief. One guy named Neil, who was at least twenty years older than me, had come in several times to both Bogart's and Henry's. He was married and didn't once question that I might not actually want to go out with him outside the club. He had a weird mixture of entitlement and naiveté. Neil even told me he was pursuing Brooklyn from Bogart's—who was only twenty—but he said she was so busy working all the time that they hadn't gotten a chance to get together. It was clear that I could have kept him as a regular for a while the way she had, but after a few times of him trying to convince me to go out with him and me making polite excuses, I laid it straight that it was not going to happen ever. I was too irritated by the assumption that it was somehow inevitable.

One time, a younger guy started a conversation by asking me out. I laughed and said, "But I don't know you." I started to talk to him, but about a minute into the conversation, he asked me out again and got immediately defensive that I would not commit to it. Most of the time, I could make a guy back off by saying, "A lot of guys ask me out. I just met you, so how do I know you're different from all the other guys who come in here?" That would make him consider things from my perspective. But this young guy responded by telling me, in a serious tone, that it was obvious that he was different and that I was mean. There was a certain freedom in knowing that there was nothing left to pursue with a customer, so I told him, "I am here to sell dances, not to date people. That's how it works at a strip club," and walked away.

I wish I could have said that to more people. Instead, I decided to develop a fictitious boyfriend. I knew most married strippers hid their rings and did not admit to being married, but it seemed that having a commitment to someone else would help deter the guys who wanted to "date" me—in other words, *sleep with me*. At the very least, it was a good excuse for why I couldn't go out with someone, although there were still plenty of guys who did not consider my boyfriend much of a threat. I got guys saying things like, "He doesn't have to know" or "You should still go out with me to see if you like me better."

The fake boyfriend worked best with the types of customers that strippers call "white knights." Those were the guys who thought it was their responsibility to somehow save you from a life of stripping, whether that happened by dating them or just listening to their wise words. How they reconciled that with the fact that they attended strip clubs and got lap dances was anyone's guess.

One time, a white knight tried to convince me I should be doing something better with my life. "Don't you think you should be doing something else? You know, something that contributes more positively to the world."

"I told you I was in school to become a librarian, right?"

"Well, you should get out as soon as you can. This isn't good for you."

That logic also belied the fact that many people's jobs did not actively make the world a better place. I decided I would much rather be a stripper than a telemarketer, an insurance claims adjustor, or a parking-ticket-enforcement officer.

Another white knight tried to offer me a job at his start-up company. It was some type of tech-support position that he thought I was the best candidate for because I had some experience with Linux. When I asked him what the pay was, he said he could probably only afford ten dollars an hour. I pointed out that I made a lot more money stripping. Then he began to look a little embarrassed, and I realized that he was trying to play out the fantasy of seeing me daily outside the club and was hoping one thing would lead to another.

A common question that came up in conversation with customers was, "How did you get into this?" I didn't mention my financial motivations and student loan debt. That wasn't sexy. Instead, I played up how exciting it was to live a secret double life. I said that I needed something fun to do at night to make up for how serious my days were at school. It was important to keep up the appearance that above all else, I was having a great time. I understood the role I was playing. I could never treat it like a financial transaction—that would immediately ruin the fantasy for many customers.

I no longer felt weird about telling a few lies here or there: "My real name is Sara," "I'm a stripper because I just think dancing and taking my clothes off is so fun," and "Yeah, I totally get aroused when I give YOU a lap dance." These white lies seemed like a necessary part of my job.

Some girls lied all the time, though, including exaggerating how many lap dances they had given to a guy who was not paying attention. One time, Rose and I were working with a group of guys who were at the club to party. We had gotten two of them to agree to go back to the private dance room with us, and they both got four dances each. After the dances were over, Rose jumped to telling her customer that he had gotten six dances and owed her $120. He said he wasn't sure that it had been that many, so she quickly included me in the situation. "Hey, Penelope, we just did six dances, didn't we?"

"Yeah, it was definitely six songs." I was not about to cross Rose, so I went ahead and accepted my extra forty dollars. The guys did not put up a big fight but nevertheless didn't look completely convinced that they had really gotten six dances. Afterward, Rose was quick to laugh with me about it and tell me I should do that all the time.

I suspected those guys would not be back in the club to see us. I met plenty of guys who came in with the assumption that I was automatically going to try to rip them off because they thought that was what strippers did by nature. Girls like Rose were not helping get rid of that stereotype.

There were fewer girls kissing their customers in the private dance room at Henry's than there were at Bogart's. The girls who kissed customers at Henry's were usually just passing through and only working a night here or there, plus a few who did it with their very good regulars. Overall, I had a lot fewer customers asking for kissing at Henry's.

One time when I was in the dressing room, getting ready for my shift, a day-shift girl came in, sobbing. She was quickly changing out of her dance outfit into her street clothes, and another girl naturally asked her what was wrong.

"They're saying I was having sex with some guy during a dance! It's not true! This is such BS. I would never do that!" She went on to cry and complain, slumping against the wall in defeat.

Eventually, Nick, one of the bouncers, knocked on the door and stuck his head in. "Come on Kiki. Finish gathering your stuff up— you've got to go."

"But I didn't do it! That's not what you saw!"

Nick shook his head and folded his arms. Kiki protested a few times more but eventually finished getting her shoes on, and I watched Nick escort her out the door. Although I had never seen anything like that at Henry's, I was still a little surprised that the bouncers had stopped it, told the manager, and Kiki had been fired on the spot. I was certain the bouncers would have just looked the other way at Bogart's. I was glad that it wouldn't be tolerated.

I was naturally nosy, so after I finished getting ready, I chased down Nick to learn more about what he'd seen.

He told me, "I knew what they were doing, so I went over and tapped Kiki on the shoulder and told her to get off the customer's lap. When she stood up, the guy's hard dick came out of her. There's is no doubt about what they were doing."

Although guys were asking less for "extras" inside the club, I was still receiving my fair share of solicitations for additional sexual services they wanted me to offer later outside the club. I was getting used to them, and they were starting to not bother me as much. It really depended on how someone asked. When a guy was aggressive about it as though he could talk me into it after I said no, then it was annoying. However, if someone was just feeling me out to see if I was available for more, I would politely explain that wasn't a service I provided but would be more than happy to give them another lap dance.

Initially, I couldn't understand why so many guys were looking for sex acts in a strip club. Yes, it made a lot more sense to ask me than a waitress. But at the same time, wouldn't it be more efficient to go straight to the source and call an escort service? An escort would be a sure thing, while many strippers would say no, not to mention that they couldn't leave in the middle of a shift without getting in trouble.

I came to think that some guys liked to believe that asking a stripper was somehow different from calling a full-service provider and just didn't count. I thought perhaps they didn't want to see themselves as guys who visited prostitutes but rather as guys who watched strippers—which was somehow a little more acceptable. The same psychology worked for the girls who performed tricks after hours—they could believe that they were not prostitutes but just strippers. Both sides of the transaction could then call it whatever they wanted and not have to use any terms that labeled what they were doing as prostitution.

I wondered at first why they didn't just go work for an escort service. That would have been easier than hanging out at the club for seven hours, looking for full-service customers. But then, most of the girls who slept with customers didn't do it all the time—they just did it when it was convenient, such as when they needed to make more money on a particular week. That type of sex work was also sometimes reserved for specific customers in the right situations that the girls felt comfortable with.

After enough time, I began to slowly figure out which girls were meeting with customers after work. They typically didn't work very often or weren't very good hustlers. And none of the high-earning girls did it, as far as I knew. They didn't need to. They worked fairly consistently and knew how to hustle.

One of the regular customers who habitually tried to talk me into meeting with him outside the club for paid sex was an older man who always told us he was on a fixed income. One time, he offered me a hundred dollars, and I laughed in his face. "If you're going to solicit me, at least offer more!"

Then he told me another girl had met with him for that sum, but he wouldn't say who. I didn't believe that. It was a ridiculous proposition, considering that despite the fact that he was always trying to get us to reduce the price of dances, I had made a hundred dollars off him for a set of pretty standard lap dances. One time, he told me I didn't do enough but he liked me anyway, as though that were a special compliment.

I got into an interesting conversation with a girl named Sapphire in the dressing room one night. She worked at Henry's sporadically and used to dance in Vegas. She told me how she also used to escort there and that she could make up to $3,000 a night. Then Sapphire went on to rant about how unsafe so many girls who met up with customers were. She said that they needed to make sure they told a good friend whatever they were doing and where they were going so she could check in at a specified time, if the girl failed to report back. The best way was to have a bouncer like the one she'd had in Vegas, who'd driven her around to her various jobs throughout the night.

One time, Autumn and I were talking to two guys who had come in, one of whom had made it very clear to us upfront that he wanted someone to get him off. First, we suggested he call a 1-800 number, but for whatever reason, he didn't want to do that. Then he asked us if there were any girls at Henry's we could find to help him out. Autumn suggested he drive over to Bogart's and ask for Margo. The guy took her advice very seriously, and as soon as the two guys left the club, we crouched over in laughter. I didn't know so many people at Henry's also knew about Margo.

For the rest of the night, Autumn and I just kept joking about how Margo was going to react when those two guys came in looking for her because some girls from Henry's had sent them. Then we considered that she might not even blink but would just think, "Of course," without another thought.

Without realizing it at the time, I think we were laughing at Margo because we had internalized the belief that sex work that involved more contact than stripping was somehow "worse." Despite doing sex work ourselves, we had internalized the social standard that sex acts that were criminalized were more wrong. It took a while for me to overcome those biases.

I kept hearing stories from Autumn, Rose, Megan, Heaven, and others about "how it used to be." The clubs used to be busier—a girl had to hustle a lot harder to make her money these days. I had the sense that I had missed out on the good old days when money was easy and plentiful. Part of me wished I had gotten over my taboos about stripping when I was eighteen, because I could have made a lot more money back then. I kept hearing stories about how a girl could start her shift whenever she felt like it, pay off her house fees, and still consistently make at least $500 a night, all while doing lap dances with less mileage.

One time, I caught Autumn complaining in the dressing room when she was having a bad night. "I used to cry if I didn't make $400 by midnight, and now the night's almost over, and I've only made, like, $200 dollars."

Most of the girls attributed the decreased strip club attendance to the hit the Michigan economy had taken from the decline in the auto industry. In 2005–2006, Michigan had the lowest unemployment rate in the country, and the subsequent drop in employment was due to the many layoffs at Ford, General Motors, Chrysler, and their parts affiliates throughout the state. Everyone said we had too many eggs in one basket and desperately needed to diversify Michigan's industries. The girls were all hoping that if the economy picked back up, the clubs would get busy again, and they'd start making the money they used to make.

I was beginning to suspect that this was not likely. Online message-board speculation among strippers pointed to the increased availability of Internet porn and webcam girls as a probable cause of the decline in the stripping industry nationwide. The decline was happening everywhere. There were other ways to get titillated without even having to leave home, and the prices were getting cheaper and cheaper. Someone didn't have to be an expert to know that what girls were providing for free online had increased significantly since the advent of Internet porn. Porn sites took the chance that a viewer's interest would be piqued and they would be willing to pay a small monthly fee for more hardcore videos. Consequently, more men wanted more bang for their buck in strip clubs as well. They tipped a lot less on the stage than they used to. Many expected more during a lap dance, and others would try to negotiate for deals to get more dances for a smaller amount of money than twenty dollars a dance.

The sexual-entertainment industry had become oversaturated in general. There were more and more women who were willing to perform the whole deal online, and there were more women willing to strip. The high earnings that strippers had experienced in the '80s and '90s had a lot to do with the fact that fewer women were willing to take their clothes off for money. Stripping was beginning to lose some of its stigma, and for some girls entering the business, it was perceived as exciting and glamorous. In short, more women were working in the clubs, and fewer customers were coming in.

Many of the girls I worked with had noted that the expected lap dance mileage had increased significantly over even just the past five years. It seemed inevitable that it was only going to keep increasing.

The longer I worked, the more local clubs there were that were notorious for having just about everything available in the back room. My own experience indicated that Bogart's was heading in that direction as well. I figured Henry's could only maintain being a relatively clean club for another few years at the most.

12

------◄◦►------

The momentum of any given night could really vary. A good night would keep getting better and better. The club was full and dances were easy to get. The best was walking out of the private dance room and finding a customer waiting because he already had his eye on me. Then I was back in the dance room, essentially making twenty dollars every three minutes, because strip club DJs deliberately only played songs that were on the short side. For some reason, the busier and the more inaccessible a girl seemed, the more appealing she was to customers—once the ball was rolling, it kept rolling.

A bad night, on the other hand, could happen just as often. The trick was not to let yourself get too down if the night started slowly, because there was always potential for money if the club got busier later. Sometimes, that was easier said than done, though. If there was no momentum in the first few hours of the night, it was hard to generate the energy later on.

One night, I just couldn't make it happen. Two hours had passed since the shift had started. It was very slow and a group of pretty new girls had come in to work, giving us an unusually large number of girls to compete with on a weeknight. They were getting all the dances, and I was losing my confidence. Since there were no customers open who weren't dead ends, I was sitting at the bar drinking with Curly, one of the daytime bouncers who'd stayed to hang out.

He was keeping me somewhat distracted from how badly the night was going, but I was beginning to get a sinking feeling that I just couldn't do it that night. I was overly intimidated by the group of new girls, and I couldn't imagine jumping back into the game if the club actually got busier. My sense of dread kept mounting, and I began deliberating about throwing in the towel for the night. I had already paid my house fee and I had become convinced I wasn't going to make it back anyway. I felt a greater and greater urge to leave before I began to get even more frustrated and upset. I recognized that my state of mind was not conducive to making money, so I finally decided to just cut my losses.

I went and talked to Fred about leaving early. We were supposed to stay the whole shift, and there was supposed to be some sort of penalty if we left early. I told him I hadn't made any money yet, so he told me I could go without any issue, mainly because I had proven to be pretty reliable, but I shouldn't make a habit of it.

I quickly went to the dressing room and got into my street clothes. By the time I got into my car, I realized I had been crying. I felt weak and pathetic, like a fraud who wasn't strong enough to hack it. As I drove down Michigan Avenue on my way back to Ann Arbor, I felt a strange, overwhelming urge to call my mother and confess everything. I was having a breakdown, and somehow that seemed like the most natural thing to do: call Mom. Plus, I wasn't thinking straight at that point.

Before I knew it, I had dialed my parents' number and my mom had picked up.

"Mom, I have something to tell you."

"What is it? What's wrong?" She could hear me sobbing into the phone.

"I know I said I wouldn't do it, but I've been stripping for the last four months. I'm driving home right now because I had a bad night."

"Oh no… " She sighed.

It couldn't have been a complete surprise. After all, I had been "joking" about it to them throughout the summer before. No one had taken my childish threats seriously, though.

After she had collected herself, her first response was, "Don't tell your father." That was pretty easy to agree to.

She listened to me babble on about how it was the only way I could make ends meet. I couldn't get a waitressing job, and my library job didn't pay very much—plus the hours varied and weren't enough—but I needed to keep it if I was going to get the experience I needed to get a job as a librarian after graduation. Overall, she handled it better than I thought she would. I felt oddly relieved to have gotten such a big secret off my chest. I went home, got into bed, and commenced a marathon of Stargate SG-1.

Later, I found out that my departure had created a little drama. I had gotten messages on my phone from Heaven, who said she was worried about me when I left abruptly. I called her back later and told her I was fine, just having a bad night. I got over my little breakdown and went back to work a few nights later. I found out when I got there, from Nick, the bouncer, that Heaven had been freaking out all night after I left because she thought Curly and I had left together to hook up just because we had been talking before I left. Apparently, she had spent the night expressing her worry to everyone who worked there. The story was that Heaven had slept with Curly once and subsequently became obsessed with him, but he wasn't interested in her. He considered their hookup a mistake because, like a lot of people, he thought Heaven wasn't emotionally stable.

Curly was also easily thirty years older than me. I thought that fact made it obvious that I wouldn't have hooked up with him, but Heaven was so infatuated with him that she naturally thought other women wouldn't be able to resist his sex appeal. She wasn't there the night I returned, but I made sure to have a talk with her the next time we both worked. I didn't want everyone else at Henry's thinking I had a thing with Curly because of Heaven's paranoid worries. Before that had happened, I had given Heaven the benefit of the doubt when other people bitched about how crazy she was.

The odd thing about talking to Heaven was that despite her worries, she gave off nothing resembling anger or hostility toward me. I told her point-blank that Curly and I did not meet up and that I went straight home. I also tried to make it patently clear that I had no interest in him at all. I hoped she believed me, but it was hard to tell since I knew she interpreted the world around her so differently.

That silly little drama helped distract me somewhat from my fear of returning to the club and trying to hustle again. Luckily, I was able to just go back and not let my bad night affect future nights.

I continued to talk to my mom over the next few weeks and was beginning to feel that she had accepted that I would be stripping for the time being and that was just how it was. Then she called me with a determined plan to make me quit. She said she wanted to come visit and buy me a suit and also give me some money she had set aside. It technically would have been enough for me to live on for the next few months, when my final semester ended, but it still didn't solve my long-term problem of being ultimately $80,000 in debt.

I continued to tell her that wasn't enough to stop me and I hadn't called her to get her to bribe me into stopping in the first place. She kept begging me to accept and then went on to talk about how important having a nice suit would be for the interviews I would be going on soon. In her mind, that suit was the answer to all my problems. The more I tried to tell her no, the more desperately she continued to insist that I had to do this.

I finally decided she couldn't handle the truth, which was fine. I shouldn't have expected her to in the first place. That had been a residual effect of my former feeling that I had to be radically honest with people. In a moment of weakness, I had freaked out, and now I had to undo the distress I had caused her.

I considered quitting just to avoid my mom's grief, but then I would be left with the feeling of helplessness in the face of my debt. Overall, since stripping had entered into my life, I was actually happier. I felt as though I had more overall control of my life and finances. I knew the solution I had come to would seem ridiculous to most people, but it was working for me for the time being. I'd had my bad night, but I had gotten over it quickly. Before deciding to attack my debt by stripping, I'd had many more bad nights of feeling sorry for myself.

So, I called my mom and told her I would stop. In doing so, I became an even bigger liar. I felt bad about it, but it was what she needed to hear to feel okay, just as stripping was something I needed to continue to do to feel okay.

She came out to visit me the following weekend. I cleaned my room and had her sleep on my bed while I slept on the couch in the living room. We went to the mall, and she bought me a suit at The Limited. I even got the pants tailored because my legs were still a little too short even for the petite pants. It was the first time anything had ever been tailored for me. I was used to walking around in pants that were too long for me.

I took her around the university's campus, and we went out to eat a few times. Overall, it was a pleasant visit. The Sunday my mom left, I went to work at Henry's that night. After I deposited the check she had given me, I immediately wrote a check of the same amount out to Citibank and sent it in the mail. My private loan was a little smaller than my federal loans, but the interest rate was going up. At that point, my interest rate was 6.7 percent—it would eventually get higher than 8 percent before the financial crisis of 2008 finally brought interest rates down.

I'd like to say that disclosing what I was doing to my mom was the only stripping breakdown I had, but it was merely the first. The next time it happened, I wasn't at work. I was on the Internet, which could have been even worse if I'd managed to finish the email I accidentally sent.

I had been brooding in my room, feeling sorry for myself and thinking again about how unhelpful my experience at the School of Information was, especially in light of the sheer amount of money I owed and what I had been doing to rectify that situation. Recently, the dean of the school had done a guest lecture in my Management of Special Libraries class. His topic was "Having the Administrator Gene." Basically, the point of it was that some people were just natural leaders, which made them special, as he clearly thought he was. He also insisted on describing his whole idea as though there were some actual evidence for its genetic basis. The entire thing was pretentious and kind of douchey and definitely not remotely scientific.

The dean had a reputation around the school for being unavailable and self-important. That was the first time I had ever seen him present anything, and it was my fourth and last semester. Ordinarily, it would be odd to have expected more contact with my school's dean, but we had fewer than three hundred students and were the smallest school at Michigan.

I was tired of the hype SI had been generating about itself, so I decided to draft an email to him with all of my gripes and then point out that SI can't be that great if one their students was a stripper. Writing this down was meant to be more of a cathartic exercise than anything else, as I did not actually intend to send it. Sometimes when I was mad, I liked to write down my thoughts in the form of an email to the person I was mad at. I would never actually send them, because I would usually be over whatever it was that was upsetting me by the next day.

It probably would have been a better idea if I had drafted my disgruntled email in a Word document and just left it there on my computer. But instead, I opened up my email, put the dean's email address in the "To" field, and began my rant. The idea was to just save it in the draft folder and perhaps think about sending it later if I still felt strongly, which I really wasn't planning on doing.

I only got the first paragraph of my rant out when I accidentally sent it somehow as I was pressing enter to start the next paragraph. I was really only warming up at that point, talking about my expectations upon entering SI, and had not yet written anything about stripping. Although I had not quite reached the ranting stage of what I was intending to write, I had made it clear that my email was not intended to be a positive one and that it was only the beginning.

I felt a little ill in my stomach and immediately knew I never would have sent that email anyway, had I finished writing it. I told Aurora what I had done, and she suggested not actually putting the person's email address in the "To" field, for future reference. That seemed obvious, after the fact. I felt pretty stupid and my anxiety about how he would receive the email began to mount quickly.

Finally, I just took solace in the fact that I had not actually mentioned I was a stripper and hoped what I had heard about the dean's avoidance of students was true. I hoped he would just ignore it because, as a student at SI, I wouldn't be particularly relevant to him. Aurora helped cheer me up, and I began to feel better. There was nothing I could do about it at that point.

In the worst-case scenario, he would think I was an annoying idiot, and at the end of the day, that really wouldn't affect me. It was unlikely he would even know who I was in person. I would be just a name to him. We did have pictures on the program website, but those were taken when I first entered, and my hair and glasses were very different. I only had a few more months to keep my head down and get out of there. That was the rationalization I created for myself, anyway.

The next day, I decided to just avoid my email as that would somehow make everything okay. If I didn't check it, there could be no repercussions. I could only keep that approach going for so long, though, because I needed to read my messages, especially when I had group projects and other school communications to keep up with.

I held my breath when I finally checked my email two days later. I quickly scrolled through my accumulated messages and found I had not gotten a reply. Just as I was about to feel relieved, though, I discovered an email from the woman in charge of career services. I was used to getting emails from her in my inbox, but they were all student-wide communications about stuff like additions to the job bank and mock interview opportunities. This one was directed specifically to me. She mentioned that the dean wanted her to contact me. It was essentially a message about how great an SI degree would prove to be and how she really wanted to meet with me to help me prepare for my job search.

That was the same woman who had previously told me she was too busy to talk to me, when I had contacted about looking for an internship. I probably did need her help, but I didn't want it at that point. I never replied.

13

---◆○◆---

uring my final semester, I was in a group with three other girls for a collection-development project. The class was taught by the program's only professor who had a focus in public libraries, and our assignment was to create a collection-development policy for a library of our choice.

A collection-development policy was a statement of a library's intentions with regard to building a collection, including how new materials would be added and old material would be weeded out. The statement would usually include the American Library Association's Library Bill of Rights. It was a great way to combat any attempts at censorship. Our group got together because we were interested in making a policy for a public library while some of the other groups were interested in doing one for academic libraries. Overall, it was an interesting project, and it was not until later on that I realized just how useful it was in professional practice.

We were allowed to choose whatever library we wanted to make a policy for, and none of us had a particular library in mind. We wanted to go for something random, so we ended up selecting the Fargo Public Library in Fargo, ND. Because of the Coen Brothers, we initially imagined that community to be a lot smaller than it actually was. We divided up the components of the policy among the four of us and then worked at putting it all together.

My partners were all a year behind me in the program because most people doing the library science concentration took that class their first year. I also discovered that the fathers of two of the girls were specialist doctors, and I realized that made a lot of sense. If a person had to pay to pursue a graduate degree in a field that didn't pay very much, it seemed to work out better if someone else was footing the bill.

I was unjustly jealous of their privilege. Although I was again feeling sorry for myself and wondering why life was unfair and all my typical whiney thoughts, I was beginning to get a better understanding of my own privilege compared to many of the girls at Henry's. That difference was amplified by the fact that Henry's was a working-class strip club, unlike some of the higher-end clubs just down the street. Despite not being able to afford the grad school I chose; I had still grown up with better economic advantages and educational opportunities than the girls I worked with.

It was a bit of a stretch for my parents to afford orthodontic work for me, but that was the norm in the town we lived in, so they splurged on it. I never did a survey, but I didn't think any of the girls I worked with had access to orthodontic work in their early teens. I did meet one stripper with braces, but she was bankrolling them herself.

At the end of the day, I had a safety net in my parents that most of the women I worked with did not have. Although I still had my outstanding debt, I knew that if I had no money, I could always move home, as I had the summer before.

I also had the major advantage growing up in a home and a community where going to college was normalized. It was always something I knew I would do. There were plenty of examples of people around me who had gone to college to get four-year degrees, including my own mother, and they were my models for what I could attain in life. For people who'd grown up in poverty, it was completely normal not to know anyone who had gone to college and consequently not even entertain that as a possibility.

One time in the dressing room, when the night had just ended, all the girls were talking about what they were planning on doing when they got home, mostly in the vein of sleeping or continuing to party. I mentioned that I still had schoolwork to do.

Rose then prophesized emphatically, "You're smart, girl. Make your money, and get out of here. We're all going to be hearing from Penelope one day. She's going to write a book about all of us here at Henry's some day and then forget all about us."

"I can't write a book! No one even knows I'm a stripper."

"Then write a book about something else. Girl, you can do whatever you want." I appreciated Rose's confidence in me, but I couldn't imagine disclosing my secret life to the world at that point. Whether anyone would want to read it would be another matter, but the real takeaway from her remarks was that I had the educational background to write a book if I wanted to.

I was also made aware of my privilege one day when I was talking to Megan. I told her how I had lost my social security card and then I couldn't find my driver's license. "Luckily, I still have my passport in case I need an ID."

She wrinkled her nose at me. "You have a passport?" as if that was one of the weirdest things she had ever heard.

"Yeah, why not?"

"Ooo, so fancy." She went on to tell several of the other girls that I had a passport as though it was breaking news. At that point, my coworkers had accepted me, so no one thought ill of me for it. None of the other girls thought my passport was quite as bizarre as Megan did, but it was still a reminder of our different life circumstances.

I had gotten the passport when I was twenty so I could go to Madrid for a week at the end of the summer between my sophomore and junior years. I had been fantasizing about studying abroad for a semester but realized that I would never be able to afford it. Then a Spanish friend invited me to visit her at her family's house during our summer break. It was by far the cheapest way for me to go to Europe, so I worked a second waitressing job all summer to save up the money for the airfare. Even though I paid for it all myself, I had the advantage of being exposed to a wider variety of people in college and making friends from other countries. I knew people who traveled internationally. Going to other countries wasn't some wild, unattainable phenomenon for me.

It didn't matter how much money Megan made—she was not likely to get a passport and engage in international travel. That kind of thing wasn't normalized for her, and she probably had very few examples in her personal life of people who had traveled overseas—other than to go fight a war in Iraq or Afghanistan.

A discussion of class privilege in a strip club would be incomplete without addressing some of the race dynamics I encountered. If there was one thing I could say about Henry's, they at least did not discriminate in their hiring practices. I had heard from Black strippers that there were upscale clubs that would turn them away because "I'm sorry, we already have a Black girl." Because I'm sure those clubs turned away big-breasted tan blondes when they already had too many of that "type" as well.

Although I saw the ethnically diverse group of girls get plenty of dances with white guys, I couldn't imagine they did not encounter prejudice in their conversations with some of our customers. One time, a customer complained to me that we had too many Black girls working that night. All I could think of to say was, "Why does that matter?" He didn't have an answer.

I never worked with any trans strippers who were out. I can't imagine a trans stripper who worked in one of those clubs at that time feeling safe disclosing this to the other girls. Someone like Megan might get the idea to spread it everywhere, and then all the customers would know. I'm sure some of them would be fine, but then there would be others who wouldn't be. Trans sex workers have been most at risk of violence, and this is heightened for trans sex workers of color.

I didn't know anyone who was out as non-binary during this time, in either the strip club or in my life outside the club. The last time I visited a strip club as a customer, one of my friends got a dance from a non-binary stripper who introduced themselves that way. My friend is a butch lesbian, though, so they probably felt safer disclosing that with her.

The girls I worked with who had the most difficult lives were probably the ones who did not work very often. A girl who worked regularly and was a decent hustler could make more than enough money to get by and take care of her family. For many girls, there were mental health limits on how many nights they could work as strippers within a short time period. I discovered that my limit was four nights a week. After that, I just couldn't hustle, and a fifth night would always lead to low money. I knew women who were fine working six nights a week, though. There were others who could only handle coming in a few times a month. I think they would wait until they absolutely had to come in to make money. The extra pressure of knowing they needed to make a certain amount that night had to make hustling harder.

There was a girl named Jillian who would do this. She worked about twice a month. One night, she was freaking out about how she had bills due the next day and she wasn't making anything. She kept telling me how responsible I was by coming in regularly. I didn't feel particularly responsible, and plenty of people who knew me would have argued otherwise. I probably just had a higher threshold in terms of how much customer BS I could deal with.

The girls who worked regularly usually had their own transportation to and from work. I gave a ride home to two of the more transient women, both of whom lived in motels. One girl named Jenna wanted me to stop at a friend's house on the way home. She said he was holding on to her Xanax and she needed to stop by to pick it up. I came up with an excuse about how I did not have time to make an extra stop. She started getting a little agitated about how she needed her pills, but I didn't want to stop at her drug dealer's house.

The other girl, Diamond, was notorious for asking customers to give her rides. It was a dangerous practice, but she somehow didn't see that she was potentially putting herself in unsafe situations. She could have been offering extra services, but I wasn't sure. So when she asked me for a ride home, I thought she might have been trying to play it safe for once. Then when we got to her motel, she begged me to come inside with her so she could show me to her boyfriend. She wanted to prove to him that she had gotten a ride home with another girl instead of some random guy, because he didn't believe her when she'd told him that in the past. I begrudgingly went in with her and saw the motel room where she lived with her boyfriend, three cats, and a clothing rack. She began introducing me to him as though I was her best friend, even though we really didn't know each other very well. It was thoroughly weird, and I quickly made my excuses to get going. I didn't like being her alibi.

Diamond was a good hustler too. If she had worked more, she could've easily saved up enough for an apartment, but I got the sense that her boyfriend wasn't that into her stripping. She had to convince him to let her go out and do it from time to time when they needed money.

Megan and Cherry weren't the only hustling duo at Henry's anymore—Lexus and Brittney were there as well. Brittney followed Lexus around and did whatever she said. If she got dances, it was probably only because Lexus found them for her. Or maybe it was because Lexus was allowing her to do them. I wasn't really sure, but the longer they were around, the stranger their dynamic seemed as it unfurled before me. Brittney was sweet and Lexus was dominating and kind of cold. One time, I found Brittney crying in the dressing room because her boyfriend had just broken up with her. When Lexus came in, she expressed no empathy. She told her to get off the floor and get out there and work.

Although Lexus was the alpha in her relationship with Brittney, it was clear that Lexus's boyfriend was dominant in her relationship with him. Like Dawn, she would report in to her boyfriend throughout the night about how well she was doing, and apparently, that was what he expected. One time, some asshole customer smacked her really hard on her butt during a lap dance, leaving a red hand impression on one of her butt cheeks. I was mad for her when she came into the dressing room to complain about it. The bouncers had walked the guy out, but she had every right to be pissed. Then I realized she wasn't mad that this random man had hit her but that he had left a mark, which she didn't want to have to explain to her boyfriend when she got home.

"It's not your fault. Why would he get mad?"

"He'll still be mad, and he'll say I shouldn't have let it happen."

"Well, can't you just not let him see your ass tonight?" someone suggested.

"No, he's going to want to do it. We do it every night. "

"Can't you just tell him you're not in the mood?" I asked. This was too sad.

"No. It doesn't matter."

"Even when you're on your period? If you don't feel well?"

"We always do it anyways."

"What about turning the lights off or doing it on your back."

"We always do it doggie style. That's how he likes it." She said all of this very seriously as though it were obvious.

"Girl, your man sucks. I'd never let my dude treat me that way," Autumn said, and Lexus shot her laser eyes.

I really hadn't liked Lexus before because of the way she talked to Brittney, but now I just felt bad for her. She knew how to be tough with the other girls, but she was completely controlled by her pimp-wannabe boyfriend at home. It was terrible that he would get mad at her for something abusive another man had done to her outside of her control, and her only worry was hiding it from him because they had the kind of relationship where she had to have sex with him every night.

The dynamics of Lexus and Brittney's relationship continued to get weirder as time went on. I found Brittney in the dressing room, smiling, as she counted her money one night. It was the first time I had seen her in a good mood since her boyfriend had broken up with her. She happily said, "Joe called me to check on how I was doing tonight."

"Huh? Who is Joe?"

"Lexus's boyfriend."

"Wait. He's calling you to see how much money you've made so far tonight?"

"Yes." She beamed at me.

I was tempted to then ask why that was a good thing. She was happy this Joe guy wanted to also be her pimp? What could I even do with that kind of information?

Brittney saw the perplexed look on my face. "Oh, Lexus knows, and she's fine with it. He wants to help take care of me too."

"Um, aren't you taking care of yourself by working here?"

She just shook her head, still smiling.

At the end of the day, most women went into stripping to make money—or in Lexus and Brittney's case, to make money for someone else. I didn't like the stereotype that strippers were doing it to get attention, based on some stupid Freudian interpretation of their childhoods. That really wasn't the case for the majority of the women

I worked with, but there were a few newbie strippers who were in it for something like that.

I met one woman who had just worked her first shift ever during a slow day. She was telling everyone in the dressing room about how she just wanted to do it for the one day because her boyfriend had broken up with her. Although she didn't get any dances and had to pay the house fee, dancing naked on the stage for strangers had made her feel better. I probably asked her too many questions, trying to understand where she was coming from, but she was certain that her day of stripping had helped her get over her boyfriend.

Once, a girl who worked at Henry's from time to time, along with some other clubs, was talking about how excited she was that Girls Gone Wild was in town. She really wanted them to pick her so she could flash for a free T-shirt then have her image used for free in Girls Gone Wild 18, or whatever number they were on at the time. I didn't understand her motivation, either. Part of the reason I liked stripping much better than doing some type of internet "modeling" was because there was no record of it. Even though I took my clothes off for money, I couldn't relate to wanting to do it for free or having my image out there where anyone could find it.

The girls whose motivation I understood the least, however, were some of the strip club waitresses. They may have made more at high-end clubs, but the waitresses at Henry's often only made minimum wage. Because they were actually considered employees—unlike the strippers, who were contractors—the club was legally required to pay them more than the meager $2.65 they made an hour if their total earnings, including tips, did not add up to minimum wage. There were girls who had worked there for years. Why not go work at a regular restaurant, where they would probably make more money? Although they didn't perform onstage or give lap dances, they still had to deal with gropey customers who would proposition them.

Most of the waitresses I talked to said they could never strip, and they usually spoke in such a way as to indicate that they thought they were better than that. A lot of them didn't seem to mind the hustling element of the strip club, though. Although they weren't trying to hustle lap dances, they were trying to hustle drinks and additional tips.

There was an extra-creepy guy who came in often near the beginning of the night. I learned quickly that he wasn't worth talking to because he did not get dances or even tip the stage. But one day, I did observe him putting his hand up a waitress's skirt as he very slowly handed her dollar bills. I guess he really wanted to get the most from each dollar, and the strippers just weren't doing enough for him onstage.

It was not uncommon to hear about the waitresses telling customers sob stories to get bigger tips. One time, a quite naive regular of mine—yes, there were naive strip club customers!—was worried that he should have tipped his waitress better because she had told him she really needed medicine for her baby. He had already handed her forty dollars. I had to explain to him that she was really looking for money for pills for herself, which I knew because she was complaining about running out earlier. He was shocked that someone would make that up, and I had to assure him that he didn't do anything wrong by not randomly handing twenties over to her. I felt a little bad for that guy. He really was easy picking for a shark.

Megan's sister was also a waitress in the club. Like Megan, it was probably the only job she'd ever had. She also spent a lot of time at their home, watching Megan's children. She had somehow developed a special relationship with one of my regulars whom I always had trouble making conversation with. He liked me because he was into armpits, and he appreciated that I didn't think it was weird, but when we were just sitting at a table, trying to chat with him was like pulling teeth. Regardless, this guy and Megan's sister had a bond, and he took her to Las Vegas. It was a really big deal at the time, because she hadn't been farther than Ohio in her life. Everyone was so excited for her.

One waitress had two children with a bouncer named Ed. They had been together years before, and he was married to someone else by the time I worked at Henry's. I knew a lot of girls who thought he was really sexy, but I didn't understand the appeal. Ed had a shaved head, a goatee, and full tattoo sleeves. He didn't say very much, so a lot of girls thought he had this hot, mysterious thing going on. When I finally had my first conversation with him, he seemed really mumbly, and I couldn't understand what he was trying to say.

Cherry was the only other regular girl who didn't get his appeal. She told me that although Ed was married, Megan and a few other strippers had slept with him. Then the bombshell hit that he had gotten another waitress pregnant. Although I heard there was a little bit of "I told you so" from the first mother of his children to the recently knocked-up waitress, the weird situation did not seem to affect their friendship.

My favorite bouncer was Nick, mostly because he shot the shit with me when the club was dead. He liked me and would continually ask me out, which was annoying. I would point out to him that he should be immune to strippers after sitting at the club with them all day, every day. But he would insist he wasn't immune to me and would compliment me, saying I was smart. He also didn't seem to mind how many times I said no, and when he wasn't asking me out, he was good to talk to. Nick was filled with strip club history, having worked at Henry's for years as well as another strip club in the area. He was obsessed with mixed martial arts, and although he was not that big, I trusted him the most to handle the situation if I ever needed help with a difficult customer.

I did not trust Ray, though. Ray was a big bouncer who was related to Ed in some way. He always sat around like a bulldog with a grumpy expression on his face. He seemed perpetually pissed at tip-out time because he didn't think we were tipping him enough and would sometimes grumble under his breath when we were handing him his cash. I worried that someday a customer would do something like hit me and Ray would just sit there and shrug.

14

---◼️◻️◻️◻️---

I also encountered a slew of characters at the reference desk. One time, two guys came in with a small dead animal they had found and put into a plastic bag. They had a $500 bet with each other about whether the animal was a mole or a shrew. They had tried to stop at a veterinarian's office for a professional opinion, but none were open.

I probably should have told them that we didn't allow people to bring dead animals into the library. At least, I assumed we had a policy to that effect in place. Instead, I became curious about finding out what the animal was too, and I wanted to help them settle their bet. They asked for an illustrated book about small, rodent-like animals so they could identify their find. Instead, I searched for images online and showed them the results. I took a close look at our specimen and was able to identify it as a mole.

I did have to enforce other policies at the library, though, including our porn policy. An inevitable part of public librarianship is catching patrons looking at porn on the public computers. I've caught many patrons doing that through my career, but my first time stood out. It started when a patron came by the desk to tell me she had walked by a man at a computer who was looking at things he shouldn't. I made a walk by to see what she was talking about. There were definitely boobs on the screen.

I got the irony that I, of all people, was enforcing the porn policy, but letting patrons look at whatever they wanted was problematic with children walking around in the library. There were libraries that philosophically wouldn't block or stop patrons from looking at anything because they considered that a form of censorship. That was my initial reaction when I first heard about the filtering debate, but I found that in actual practice, letting people look at pornographic images openly in a setting with patrons of all ages walking around was more complicated (especially if your library didn't have the space or resources to set up an area for more private viewing).

I went up to the porn patron and told him he couldn't look at things like that in there and he would have to get up and leave the library. He quickly hit the back button—which led to a Google search for "naked women"—and said he wasn't doing anything wrong. I repeated that he would have to get up and go. Then he folded his arms and said he wasn't going anywhere and that he hadn't done anything. We went back and forth like that a few times. I finally got louder, and a big guy at another computer stood up and looked at him. That got the man to stand up, but then he proceeded to walk to the circulation desk and complain about me.

I followed him there and continued to ask him to leave. He argued that what I was saying was a disgrace to his character and that he was a Christian man who would never do anything like that. I continued to point out that I saw what he had searched for, but he insisted he was just looking for pictures of Nicole Kidman. He asked for the director's name and said he would be calling her to let her know how he'd been treated, and then finally left the building.

He never did call the director. I was a little curious about what he would have actually said to her. Most porn patrons were not that difficult. They were mostly embarrassed and wanted to leave as quickly as possible. Some denied it, but they would still leave for the day.

Sometimes, there wasn't an answer to a patron's question, and I had to come up with the closest approximation possible to what they wanted. They could have been looking for information that didn't exist or asking something no one knew the answer to. And sometimes they had a view of the world that just didn't match with reality.

A guy once asked me for the addresses of England, France, and "Arelan," and it took me a while to realize he meant Ireland. He wanted to write letters to them about something he clearly thought was very important. I knew better, at that point, than to ask what he wanted to write to them about. I tried explaining to the man that those were entire countries and did not have single addresses, which was a point he had not considered. So I suggested we get the addresses of their heads of state. I gave him the addresses of the offices of the presidents of France and Ireland, but we ran into a snag with England. I told him England did not have a president but a prime minister. For some reason, when he realized the prime minister was Tony Blair, he did not want to write to him. He wanted someone else, another address. I tried to explain that there was no one else who was "in charge" or would be representative of the entire country. For lack of a better address to fit his criterion, I suggested the Queen, but he didn't want her either. I then had to go into the entire structure of the British government and how Parliament consisted of a House of Commons and a House of Lords and how those two operated quite differently from the House and Senate in the US. Finally, he determined that he wanted the House of Commons, so I suggested the addresses of the Speaker or Leader, but he wanted everyone in the House of Commons to get his letter without having to send more than one letter. So I got him the postal address for the entire House of Commons.

There was one guy who smelled heavily of gasoline every day. It was easy to forget he was in the library, because when he would come in, he would go straight to the quiet study area at the back of the building. When we announced we were closing, he would exit the building, leaving a strong smell of gasoline in his wake. We were surprised no one complained about the odor, but people who encountered him probably found somewhere else to sit and study.

My coworkers and I tried speculating what he could be doing to smell like gasoline every day. Was he sleeping in a shed with a gasoline spill and had gotten so desensitized to the smell he no longer noticed it? Was he doing it on purpose trying to ward people off? What if someone lit a cigarette in his vicinity?

One of the funnier patron interactions I had was when another librarian and I were shushed by a young woman sitting by a nearby table. She was studying and apparently thought we were talking too loudly at the reference desk. We reacted by laughing and then trying to stop laughing. Whenever I told people I was studying to be a librarian, one of the first stereotypes people referenced—besides the fact that I must love the Dewey Decimal System—was that I liked shushing people all day. I would always proudly say I had never shushed anyone. Most librarians had experienced being shushed by a patron, though, and I would go on to be shushed by several more myself.

I was twenty-four when I started at the Suburban Library, and I had a few older patrons who were pretty sure I was too young to help them with their questions. Sometimes, an older person came to the desk and ended up gravitating toward the other librarian over me. But one time I was at the desk with another library aide who was my age, and the lady who approached us just kept looking back and forth at both of us as though she didn't know what to do. I finally asked her if we could help her, and she asked if there were any adults in the library she could talk to with her question. Afterward, we speculated that she probably thought we were teenagers. I had to imagine that to people over a certain age, most people under twenty-five probably didn't look that different from sixteen-year-olds.

My favorite patron was a woman named Laura. Laura came to the library often to hang out in the children's section, get books about her hero—Raven Simone from *That's so Raven*—and use the computers. Laura had Down syndrome and was extremely polite and unnecessarily apologetic whenever she came up to the desk to ask us a question about something she was doing at the computer. Usually, she would say, "I'm sorry I forgot. I'll try to remember next time." I would assure her that it was perfectly fine and she had nothing to apologize for. We were there to help her whenever she needed it.

I really appreciated Laura's determination and wished she could have served as a model of persistence for the many other adult patrons I encountered who were hostile or defeatist about everything they did not understand at the computer. Too many people got extremely frustrated and gave up when the computer did not do what they wanted it to on their first try. I also heard too many people tell me things like, "Oh, I'll never learn to do this. I don't want to ever have to use a computer, but I have to use it for a form someone is making me fill out." Laura was patient, and over time, I watched her get better and better at using the computer and finding whatever she wanted on the Internet.

I would often ask my fellow librarians if they needed help with anything during quiet periods when the library wasn't busy and there weren't many reference questions. I didn't get many additional responsibilities in the beginning, and in retrospect, I was really underutilized. At the next library I worked at, I was always happy to take advantage of student help. There was so much to do and more that could be done to better improve services to the public. In the beginning, when I was looking for things to do, I was usually assigned the task of making a bibliography. I would put it into the form of a bookmark for patrons to use so they could find out more about what we offered on that specific subject.

One time, we found out that two of the toys that had been loaned out to children had been recalled because they contained lead—a heavy metal that is toxic when ingested. We did not know which children had selected those particular toys, because they were two of many different types in a bin for the children to pull from. I was given the task of calling forty kids' parents to try to find out which two had selected those toys.

I was the obvious candidate for this terrifying task because I was newest employee and was always offering to help. I had forty people to call, and I imagined that at least some of them would be pretty angry that the library might have given their children lead toys. I was dreading making the first call. In order to prepare myself, I wrote out exactly how I would—gently—break the news and what questions I would ask each parent to try to find out who had the offending toys.

This had the potential to be a horrifying experience, but I got ridiculously lucky. The first house I called, the mother who answered the phone seemed perfectly understanding and quickly realized, as I described the toys, that her daughters had both of them. I asked her if she could bring the toys back to the library so we could dispose of them for her. I also told her that her daughters should come back in and pick out another toy. She said she would and told me to have a nice night. I was happy to quickly report to the children's librarian that I was done with the task she had given me.

Around April, I began putting in applications for my first full-time professional position. Ideally, I wanted to work in the Chicago area because I still had many friends there, but I started out by being very open to working in a wide variety of places. My main criterion as I sorted through job postings was that I wanted to live in a major metropolitan area. For one thing, I had trouble imagining myself living anywhere rural. For another, I was planning on continuing to strip a few nights a week, and in order to do that, I needed to live somewhere with a variety of clubs to pick from. So far, stripping hadn't allowed me to attack my student loan debt with quite the vigor I initially imagined. I would need to keep going if I was ever to get it down to something manageable. I felt as though my life really couldn't start till it was gone.

Whenever I saw a viable job posting, I looked up what the strip club culture was like in that area, based on club reviews and online reports from other strippers. I sent my applications out in batches and tried to make unique cover letters for each library I applied to, emphasizing my enthusiasm for public service.

I started with a few phone interviews. I had one with the New York Public Library but never heard back from them. I think the "interview" was only to get in their applicant pool because it is such a large system, but still never heard anything one way or the other. I had another with the King County Library System that seemed to go well, and they offered a second interview. They gave me the option to either do it by phone or fly out on my own dime and do it in person. That was kind of a hard choice. I could have afforded to fly out to Seattle and back, but part of me thought that was the wrong answer, based on the way they phrased the question. I opted for a second phone interview, which seemed okay, but I eventually got a rejection letter from them. I wondered if that had been the wrong answer and if flying out for an in-person interview really would have made a difference by making me look serious about wanting to work in their library system. I could just as easily have flown out, though, and still not gotten the job.

I also had a phone interview with a library in a smaller community west of Los Angeles. I messed that up when the director asked me if I had any other skills that would benefit their library, and I answered that my online research showed a large percentage of their community was Hispanic, and I told her I had some Spanish language skills. That was an exaggeration because my Spanish was only getting rustier. But the real issue with this assertion, which the director quickly pointed out to me, was that the majority of their population had been there for several generations, and most spoke English fluently. I obviously did not know much about Southern California demographics and would not be a good candidate for their library—it was definitely a stupid-white-person move to assume that a large Hispanic population didn't speak English.

One of the first in-person interviews I did was for the Ann Arundel County Public Library. They had several open positions for entry-level librarians and offered $200 travel stipends for the interviews, so I flew out to Baltimore that morning and flew back that night. The stipend covered most of my airfare, but I did have to pay for the long cab ride to and from the main county office building, where the interviews were being held. It was in a small, wooded area not near much of anything. Once I arrived, I had plenty of free time before my interview started, but there was nowhere to go. I wandered a little ways into the woods and smoked cigarettes while talking to friends on my phone. I had been hoping to not be seen smoking or come into the building with the obvious smell wafting off me. One of the interviewers did come out looking for me, though, which was pretty embarrassing. I already felt self-conscious about smelling like a chimney, and then when I was brought inside, I discovered that four people were interviewing me. For some reason, that really threw me for a loop, and I awkwardly fumbled on some questions that should have been easy.

I did get one interview in the Chicago area at one of the suburban public libraries. I was interviewed by the head of their Adult Services Department. The beginning of the interview seemed to go well. We bonded over having gone to the same high school and discovered we had both been on the swim team. But as the interview progressed, I saw that although she responded well to my answers regarding my reference experience, she seemed disappointed that I didn't have more experience with collection development or conducting and organizing library programs. I drove straight back to Ann Arbor after the interview, which gave me plenty of time to think about what else I needed to start doing to get hired somewhere. I would have to get more proactive at Suburban. Instead of asking for things to do, I would need to start suggesting things I could do.

I didn't intend to at first, but I began collecting all of my rejection letters. I tried to pretend I was doing it because I thought it was funny, but it was probably a self-defeating thing to do. I also got irrationally angry at receiving rejection letters from jobs I didn't even interview for. Some people appreciated the gesture because it let them know the job was no longer available, but to me, it seemed unnecessary. I didn't expect to get a job if I didn't get an interview for it, so there was no need to further emphasize my rejection.

Meanwhile, my program was drawing to a close, and I was doing whatever I could to get my work done. I had developed the bad habit of not paying attention during a lot of my lectures. It really depended on who was speaking and what they were talking about. I had begun the program sitting attentively with a notebook and pen but saw how progressively more and more of my classmates would bring their laptops to class. Once I started bringing mine in, it was all downhill after that. I either worked on other assignments or messed around reading stuff on the Internet. I was hardly the only person with that problem, though.

In my information visualization class, I once used the lecture time to get another assignment done. Perhaps I had been typing too aggressively. One of my classmates raised her hand to ask the professor if anyone's points were going to be deducted for not paying attention that day. Then she looked pointedly at me. That particular class included a participation element as part of the grade, and I had already raised my hand and shared my thoughts, thus ensuring my points. My professor responded that everyone had been participating enough, so no one had to worry about point deductions. I couldn't tell if she had not caught on to what the student was referring to or just didn't feel the need to address it.

I was too negative, and things like that would help justify my bad attitude. We weren't graded on a curve, so my participation points would not affect anyone else's grade. For whatever reason, that girl wanted to shame me and try to get points taken away from me. Maybe it would have made her own participation points feel more special.

Wanting to wrap up the semester didn't stop me from being rebellious about policies or procedures I did not agree with in class. In one class, we had to give presentations and our grades would be a combination of the professor's grade and those assigned by our peers; everyone would get their classmates' feedback later. I was a horrible public speaker and the anxiety of receiving the judgment of my peers did not help my confidence. I decided the best way to handle that was to give every single person in my class all the points possible for their presentations—because I really didn't consider it my business to grade them. I wrote "Good job!" enthusiastically on all of their comment sheets. I was also very vocal about how I thought this was the best approach and got one of my friends in the class to do it too.

Near the end of the semester, I was also getting a little careless about my secret identity with my classmates. I had already told two of my friends in the program what I was up to. They were people I had a lot of group projects with and also hung out with outside of class. I trusted them, so it had made sense to tell them.

Then one night at work, I got a call from a girl named Karen who had been in my collection-development group project. I had to write a group paper with her for another class. Three of us were supposed to be writing different sections of the paper. She was calling to see if I had seen the email from the guy who was supposed to write the last section of our paper. Both she and I had already emailed our sections to everyone, and apparently this guy had responded that the parts we had written seemed to cover so much that he didn't have anything to add, and we should submit the paper as it was. Karen got mad and already emailed him back, saying we did in fact need the last part of the paper, but she was not expecting a reply as the full paper was due the next day.

My first reaction was to say what I was thinking: "Ugh, I have to work till two and won't be home till three to even work on this. And he wants us to finish the paper, because he doesn't feel like it?"

"Where are you working?" she asked. I had never mentioned I had any other job than the one at Suburban to most of my classmates.

I could have just lied, but at that point I just didn't care. "I work at a strip club. I am a stripper... making money for school."

Karen paused. "What are we going to do about this paper?"

I laughed and then told her I would take care of it when I got home. I didn't want Karen writing any more of the paper than she already had. She had previously demonstrated poor writing skills to me in our other class together, and I already knew I would have to edit her part before we could put it together for submission.

When I saw her the next day, everything was normal along with our mutual annoyance at our groupmate for not doing his work. She never acknowledged that I told her I was a stripper, and I was kind of surprised by that. I could tell that Karen had lived a sheltered life, and I was pretty sure she had never met a stripper. People usually had a strong reaction to the news or expressed curiosity. Perhaps she just decided to ignore it.

I bumped into her at the grocery store a few months later and we stopped to chat and catch up. I alluded to the fact that I was working a lot and how I was up late all the time. I kind of wanted to see if she would take the bait, but she wasn't going to go there.

I didn't attend my graduation ceremony. I wasn't that excited about my degree, and I didn't feel as if I had a lot to celebrate. I'd already gotten the experience of dressing up in a robe and walking across a stage at my undergraduate graduation. Instead, I worked that night and made good money.

15

I don't remember exactly what made me decide to get fake nails. They were a stereotypical part of the stripper uniform I had not adopted at the beginning because I thought they were too conspicuous. As with tanning, I thought people would be suspicious of me if I got fake nails. I'd never been interested in them before I started stripping. Maybe it was because most of the girls I worked with had them, and I subconsciously succumbed to peer pressure. I had initially seen no point in them—I just put clear nail polish on and called it a day. Then one day I decided to try acrylic French tips and started getting them filled every few weeks.

In a way, they were symbolic of the transformation I was making into a more serious stripper. I was getting bolder, and I no longer felt like a lost little girl when I went in to strip. I was more confident, and I knew what I had to do to make my money. Fake nails seemed like the natural next step. I was becoming one of the high earners at Henry's and I was well past any fears about whether I could continue to cut it. I was also less afraid of someone in my real life randomly finding out about what I was doing. By the time I graduated, I had managed to go seven months with no one finding out, and it seemed unlikely that they would after that.

I had been doing progressively better at Henry's. I had begun recording my earnings in an Excel spreadsheet every night when I got home. Being accountable to my Excel sheet helped me make more money. If I hadn't earned a lot on a particular night, I would think about having to record a smaller amount than I was happy with and it would give me the extra incentive to generate enthusiasm and talk to more customers. By June of that year, I had reached my peak. I averaged $350 a night and when I checked in with Nick at the door to the private dance room, I could see that I often had the most dances recorded or was at least in the top three earners for any given night.

I was beginning to worry less about my library job search and considered that I could continue to strip full-time for longer than I was initially planning. I began to think my library career could wait a year or two and maybe I could just keep making money and tackling my debt. I had been spending a lot of time reading club reviews in different cities, and it was clear that I could probably make more working outside of the Detroit area and also have less mileage to deal with at the same time. My vague plan began to be to move back to Chicago after my lease was up at the end of summer and try some of the clubs there until I found one I liked.

I was getting nothing but rejections from the libraries I had been applying to, and I seemed to be getting fewer and fewer rejections in the club when I asked guys if they wanted dances. I took a break from applying for library jobs—maybe it made sense to begin shifting my focus to something that I was more successful at.

Since I had graduated, they made a new name tag for me at the Suburban library. I had the full librarian title. I did not, however, get the corresponding raise that typically went with that title. My schedule was still variable there, but I worried about leaving that library if I went to another city to strip. Even though I was beginning to focus more on stripping for the long term, I was wary about not working in a library for an extended period of time because it might be even harder to get a full-time job if I had an unexplained gap in my résumé. I considered that once I figured out what I was doing, I could still apply for part-time librarian positions. There seemed to be a disproportionately large number of those available than full-time positions anyway.

The older women I worked with continually reminded me that all strippers have a shelf life, and those who were still in the clubs working past a certain point had a harder time. That made me want to take advantage of the earning power I had before I grew old and my earning potential dissipated. A lot of those women were cautionary tales for the younger strippers in the club. We all knew we would want out before we got to that point, but not everyone had an exit plan. My plans to strip as I studied to be a librarian had shifted to just being a stripper with plans to eventually become a librarian. But I was beginning to feel wary that my plan might not be realistic. Part of me wondered if I just wanted to escape how unsuccessful and unprofessional I felt in the "real world."

I had begun thinking about what I could do to remain successful in stripping for the long term. I even entertained the idea of breast implants. I didn't see myself getting them in the near future, but I was ready to acknowledge that they were a possibility I might consider in the future, if I continued to strip for long enough. Although I had customers who told me all about how much they liked my natural breasts, I could see that the girls who had good implants did better. All the women who posted about their experiences getting augmentations on stripper message boards had reported making consistently better money afterward. They were also more likely to work at some of the better clubs and have opportunities for even higher earnings. I had stopped viewing my breasts as my own private intimate objects but instead as part of my uniform. I figured if I did get implants, I could always get them removed ten years down the line. Like a career as a stripper, I couldn't see myself having them forever.

I had also mostly stopped wearing my dominatrix boots. They were too cumbersome to put on and take off every night, plus they got in the way during more acrobatic lap dances. I had progressed up to eight-inch platform heels. However, the heel itself was still a little chunky. I did not want to wear stilettos for seven hours straight.

I finally accepted that I needed some way for customers to contact me to find out when I was working. I lost money when they didn't know when I was working or if I varied my schedule, which I inevitably did. Looking back, it probably would have been cost-effective to just get a second phone, but I still wasn't completely comfortable with the idea. I decided that the best way to offer communication was to give them the stripper email I had created.

I did not use this as often as I planned and only received a few emails from customers. It was 2006 and I still had customers who were not really using email yet, or at least not regularly. The email helped alleviate some of the persistence of guys who insisted they really needed to contact me, though. For that reason, I gave it to a particularly creepy dentist, who told me that his wife was also a librarian. I refrained from asking him where she worked—I did not want to know. He had been very handsy during his dances that night and had kept trying to lick me. I thought it was pretty clear by the way I responded by moving away from his gross salivating tongue, that I was not into him. Instead, as he left the club, he stopped by my stage and told me we should really find a way to continue the amazing thing that he thought had happened between us during our lap dances. I begrudgingly told him he could always come in again to see me. He wanted to know when I was working, so I told him my email out loud, hoping he would forget it.

The creepy dentist did in fact email me the next day. I decided to ignore it. I was already cultivating enough regulars and did not need him. I also felt weird about the fact that his wife was a librarian. Although he saw nothing weird about mentioning her, it made the whole idea too close to home for me. I was used to guys sometimes talking about their wives—usually they didn't, and a lot of strip club customers were single—but it was easier to imagine the dentist's wife as someone I might know. And although I maintained that I wasn't actively pursuing married men by working in a strip club where they came to me looking for some extra thrills, I didn't even want to remotely encourage a potential colleague's husband.

I was developing a few good regulars among guys who liked anything related to fetish, domination, or role-playing. Basically, I was good at entertaining the "weird" guys that some other girls might have been uncomfortable with, like my regular who liked armpits. I was my strip club's dominatrix and although I initially thought dom work and stripping would be pretty different, I found a decent number of crossover customers.

For a few of my customers, the majority of our "lap dances" consisted of me sitting on the lap dance chair and getting a foot massage. I had small feet with high arches, which was a favorite foot type among fetishists.

One particularly submissive customer, whom I had named Peter, liked to call me "Goddess." I would give him assignments such as going out and getting me something to eat or coming in wearing women's underwear under his clothes. Peter also liked to wash my boots with his tongue and act as a human ashtray. That guy still lived with his mother and would never tell me what he did for a living, although he would consistently drop $200 on me every time he came in to see me.

The other girls I worked with knew I had a higher tolerance for weird stuff. One time, Autumn sent a customer to me who'd wanted to spend his lap dances being told how she was going to take him with a giant dildo. She had only lasted a few dances doing that. She told me she was just laughing too much to keep it going. I, however, had no problem telling the guy all sorts of strange stuff. It was a nice change of pace from the usual grind. Cherry also met a man who confessed to her that he was wearing women's underwear. She went ahead and sent him to me, and he also became a regular for a while.

One time, I had a customer who was disconnected from reality. Autumn had warned me that he might be delusional, but when I walked by and he stopped me, I gave him some lap dances anyway. During the dances, he was more focused on telling me what he knew about the aliens among us than he was on enjoying himself. He also said that he suspected Autumn might be "one of them." He bought several dances and, being a sci-fi fan, I found myself asking him more and more questions about the aliens.

I reached my limit, however, with men who considered themselves dominant in a BDSM situation. I was talking to a guy once who was telling me all about his submissive girlfriends and how he liked to be their master. I thought I could go ahead and try to handle his fantasy as it involved play choking, and I understood the power dynamic he was trying to create. He complained afterward, however, that I was resisting him too much and that I had somehow not seemed authentically submissive enough. Although I didn't encounter a guy like that again, I decided I wasn't cut out for those kinds of fantasies.

Another reason I was doing so well at Henry's was that I had learned how to bounce back from rejections more quickly. My recovery was quicker if something happened to piss me off—I could compartmentalize and be upset after my shift was over. One time when I was standing at the bar talking to a customer who had initially given off a sweet and innocent vibe, I realized his hand was around my waist. I never liked it when customers did that, but I would try to put up with it for a few minutes to see if it would lead to getting some dances. In that case, the guy then quickly moved his hand down, trying to slip it into the front of my thong. I had customers try that during dances, but even then, they would usually try it more slowly to test out whether it would be okay before I began sliding their hands away. No one had ever tried this out in the middle of the bar, so I was taken by surprise. I immediately grabbed his hand, slammed it dramatically on top of the bar, and walked away.

I considered telling one of the bouncers, but I was afraid I would only get myself more upset. I might have also had to face the possibility that the bouncer would choose not to do anything about it, which would just further infuriate me. There was still a half hour left of my shift and I had more opportunities to make money. I lifted my head and proceeded sit down and talk to another guy, which led to three more dances. While I was still talking to him, though, Ray—the bouncer I distrusted most—came over and whispered in my ear that he had witnessed what had just happened and wanted to make sure it was what he thought he saw. I told him it was and he went to talk to the asshole at the bar. The guy shrugged idiotically but did not put up a struggle as Ray walked him out of the club.

I was relieved. Ray's grumblings had just been talk. He had always intended to do his job and protect us. I managed to hold off most of my fury about the whole incident until the night was over and I was in my car driving home. Ray got a big tip that night.

Although I had become one of the top earners, I tried to remain nice to any new girls who came into the club because I remembered what it had been like when I was new. One time, a new woman had started on the day shift, and some of the girls in the dressing room were calling her "truck face" because they were appalled that she had been hired. They thought she was too ugly to work there and were thinking of things to say to her to get her to not come back.

Although it was not the kindest argument, I told them if she really was as ugly as they thought, she would simply fail to make any money and stop coming in on her own. It was survival of the fittest. That kept them from saying anything to her, along with me staring down Megan and Autumn when the new woman came into the dressing room. Autumn laughed into her locker, probably thinking of all the funny things she wanted to say, but still managed to keep her mouth shut.

I didn't always succeed at being kind, though. One night, I really joined the mean-girl team. There was a new girl working that night who was doing really well with every customer she talked to. Cherry, Megan, and I were becoming more and more upset that we were not getting as many dances. We were complaining that she was too big and wore a weird-looking outfit and, we thought, must have been offering customers something extra when she asked them for lap dances.

When the new girl was called to the main stage, I commented that her legs looked weird and I thought she was wearing tights. Cherry and I kept debating with each other whether she was wearing tights, so Megan decided to just walk up to her onstage and reach out and touch her leg. Then she turned around and walked back to us, and we began snickering uncontrollably. It was obvious that we were laughing at her, and she must have known. That was a pretty bitchy thing to do.

One woman who passed through Henry's had my real name as her stage name. I almost told her that when she introduced herself to me in the dressing room, but luckily, I stopped myself. I didn't usually share my name with new girls because there was no safeguard to ensure they didn't share that information with customers. As it was, I once caught Megan giving me a funny face when she overheard one of our regular customers calling me Sara, and she barely stop herself from saying anything.

My namesake probably wouldn't have told a customer my real name out of malice but rather from not understanding boundaries. She told me she was forty—though I thought she looked younger—and had worked at every single club in the metro Detroit area at one point. The more stories she told, the more I got the sense that she had been in trouble for reasons very different from the usual extras and drugs. I figured out that she always began freaking out about something really random, like one story she told me about finding cherry pits in a locker she liked to use and wanting everyone to drop everything and help her get to the bottom of how they got there. Then she got more upset because no one saw this as an issue. These kinds of things would unsettle everyone so much that she would sometimes get banned from working at places.

Her emotional difficulties made more sense when I found her in the locker room one day crying and hugging a big container of baby wipes. Although I hadn't asked, she went on to explain that the smell of baby wipes made her think about her son, who was now a teenager. She had lost custody of him a few years earlier. She explained that her mother had gotten full custody, and I refrained from asking exactly how that had happened.

She also told me about a court case she had been involved with. She mimicked the way the prosecuting attorney kept referring to her as "Miss Wayne County" in a mocking tone.

"Wait, you were Miss Wayne County? As in, the pageant?" I was too curious not to ask.

"Yes. Oh, I was in a lot of pageants when I was younger."

I decided to believe her. I didn't think this lady had to make that up. Her life was already wild enough on its own. I wondered if she had been like this before she started stripping, or if the years of putting up with the kind of crap a girl had to deal with in a strip club had just gotten to her one day and she snapped. Although the stereotype of the aging, washed-out stripper was mostly about a premature decay in physical appearance, this woman's looks were still pretty good. It was her mental stability that was affecting her ability to do the job.

On a night when I wasn't working, she got into a fight with some other girls and was asked to not come back. I never found out the full story.

Overall, I did a pretty good job of staying out of club drama. If someone pissed me off, I kept it to myself and just avoided that person. I managed to only upset any of the other strippers a few times, and both cases were for things outside my control.

One time, I was talking to a customer at a side stage while Porsche was on the main stage. I had been commenting to the guy I was with about how beautiful she looked. Just at that moment, she looked down at us and could tell we were talking about her. She crouched down to accuse me of saying things about her and wanted to know what I had said. I told her the truth—that I had just been complimenting her—but she didn't believe me. Although she was paranoid, she also wasn't the type to start a real catfight. She just froze me out for about a week and then seemed to get over it.

Another accusation came from the mother in a mother-daughter stripping duo. They traveled to work at Henry's sometimes, driving all the way from Kalamazoo. The mother's name was Fantasia, and she was the lead hustler between the two of them. She was in her early forties, and her daughter was twenty. Fantasia would wander around the bar, trying to get dances, and when a customer said he wasn't interested, she would bring her daughter over as an alternative option. That worked sometimes, but then there were some customers who were creeped out by the idea. I could understand why a guy might not want a lap dance from someone whose mom was in the same room.

Fantasia seemed to be completely unaware that many people thought that a mother and daughter stripping together was odd. At least, she acted as though the oddity hadn't occurred to her.

One night, Fantasia came to work without her daughter. When she was onstage, a customer she had recently been sitting with called me over to come hang out with him. He complained that she wasn't taking the hint that he wasn't interested and said that he wanted to buy lap dances from me. I gave him several dances. Later, when I encountered Fantasia in the dressing room, she announced to anyone who was around that it was too bad Henry's had an asshole who stole customers from people and how that just wasn't right. She kept repeating it over and over throughout the night whenever I was within earshot of her. There was no doubt that her comments were directed toward me.

I decided to ignore her accusations. I didn't think she would take it well if I told her that the customer in question had specifically requested me. He had probably been too passive in rejecting her, and she had assumed I had swept in and taken him away because that was easier to believe.

I was particularly annoyed by her accusation because I had made a concerted effort to not mess with other girls' customers. It was completely acceptable to go up to a guy who did not already have a girl at his table, especially if he was not anyone's known regular. I saw girls doing that all the time with customers who had already agreed to get dances with me when I got off stage. Typically, the customer would just tell her he was waiting for someone else, but I certainly wouldn't begrudge the girl for trying. There was no way of knowing if a customer was waiting for someone or if he had just been talking to the last girl at his table.

Luckily, Fantasia did not hold any particular sway with the other women and did not come in very often. If a more powerful girl in the hierarchy had been pissed at me like that, I would have been screwed.

16

---◆○◆---

I liked working holidays because fewer girls showed up to work and plenty of guys still came in looking for dances. I was one of only four girls who showed up on Memorial Day, for example, and I had a line of customers throughout the night. I barely had a moment to sit down and smoke, because as soon as I would come out of the private dance room or off the stage, I would have a customer standing there, waiting for me to be available for lap dances.

Although I worked at Henry's most of the time I was stripping, I still went back to Bogart's every now and then for discount dance night on Tuesdays. Some of the high rollers I worked with at Henry's didn't like the concept of discount dance night and would never work it when we had it at Henry's on Mondays. All dances were ten dollars, which meant a girl had to do twice as many dances to make the amount of money she would make with the regular twenty-dollar dances. The fact that ten-dollar dances were so much easier to sell more than made up for that as far as I was concerned. Many more guys came to discount dance nights with the intention of buying lots of dances. I didn't have to waste so much time hustling and building up a rapport with someone in the hopes that it would lead to dances. I could almost always count on making at least $300. Even at Bogart's, there were fewer guys looking for extras during a ten-dollar dance, so Tuesdays were the only nights I could tolerate the average Bogart's customer.

When the Fourth of July fell on a Tuesday, it seemed like a good idea to go into Bogart's that night. It was the perfect combination of holiday and discount-dance-night busyness, creating a night of easy hustling. When I went in, DJ Russ pointed out that since I hadn't worked at Bogart's in a while, I would need to come in on other days, too, because they had a rule about not letting anyone work just on discount dance night. He said, though, that he would make an exception for me for just that one time. The fact that there were only five other girls at the club to start out the night probably factored into his decision.

I went about my business and, as expected, got dances easily when there were customers in the bar. The night started a little slow, so I still had some downtime near the beginning until more people came in after watching fireworks.

I also ended up wasting time with a table of older guys with Eastern European accents. One had put his arm around me and kept insisting that I stay at their table and hang out with him. I asked him if he wanted a dance, but he kept putting me off, saying there would be plenty of time for that later and that I should just stay there and hang with him. I stayed and did a round of drinks, but he still wasn't ready for a dance after I asked him again. I told him I would stop by later and tried to walk away, but he continued to hold onto me as though I were his possession. I had to physically extract his fingers from my side as he continued to insist that I stay.

The club had begun filling up and I needed to find people who were actually interested in getting dances. Later on, I passed the aggressive Eastern European man on my way to the dressing room from the private dance room. He reached out as though trying to catch me. I quickly ducked and kept walking. I decided it was another one of those situations I could wait till later to be annoyed about, because it would just interfere with my ability to stay focused on getting dances.

In the dressing room, I bumped into Gwen, one of the first girls I had gotten to know at Bogart's, about nine months earlier. She said she had been watching me and that I had become a good hustler, adding, "I still can't do it very well, but you sure know how to work it. You go make that money, girl!"

I appreciated the compliment from someone who had witnessed my very first awkward attempts at stripping and talking to customers. I realized I had come a long way.

By the end of the night, the club had really filled up. There still weren't that many girls working and I could see that I would easily be able to get dances for the rest of the songs that night, when I wasn't onstage. It was just a matter of who to go get dances from next.

When I got called up on the main stage, it was also clear that I could actually make good tips from a stage set for once. Most guys were saving their money for dances and drinks, and with most stage sets, I only made a few bucks. Maybe in the '80s and '90s, clubs had been like stripper scenes in the movies, with guys showering girls with dollar bills, but it definitely wasn't that way by the mid-2000s.

But that Fourth of July, the stage seats were filled, and guys kept holding up dollars left and right to tip me. I sauntered over to a smiley, bald biker-looking guy who was holding up a five-dollar bill. When I went down to have him place it in my thong, he asked me to come see him after my set was over. I smiled and told him I would. Then another guy with five dollars asked me to come see him as well, and I told him I had someone waiting for me but would come see him right afterward.

I managed to walk away from that stage set with about forty dollars, which was not typical, even on a busy night. As promised, I went over to the table where the smiley biker guy was sitting and I sat down. He was in his midthirties, with a shaved head and beard, and was wearing a sleeveless shirt that showed off his tan.

I WAS A STRIPPER LIBRARIAN

"I was excited when I came in the club and saw you were working," he told me. It was usually awkward when I spoke with customers who remembered me and I did not remember them.

I tried to place him. "Oh, that's funny. I'm not even usually here. I usually work at Henry's."

"I never like going there. I had a dancer rip me off once there."

"Oh, that's too bad. When's the last time you were in?"

"I haven't been there in a few years."

I hadn't met him at Henry's, so where did I know him from?

"You don't remember me, do you?" he said.

"I'm sorry. I guess I don't. You seem familiar, though. Can you give me a clue?"

"Well, I do look different than the last time I saw you. I didn't have this beard, and I recently shaved my head."

It was coming together for me by then. "Oh, now I remember you."

"Who am I?"

"You're an architect," I said hesitantly.

The Architect smiled in acknowledgement.

He had been one of my first positive experiences with a customer in my early days at Bogart's. I remembered thinking he was a nice guy and that I wished more of my customers were like him. He had gotten a bunch of lap dances from me and kept his hands to himself, and we spent a lot of time talking about *Notes from the Underground*. When he asked me out at the end, I had told him no.

"Ah, I thought I was going to stump you."

"So, you want to come get a dance and get reacquainted?" I asked coyly.

He hesitated. "Oh, I'm not getting dances tonight."

"That's too bad," I said, standing up. "I do have another customer waiting for me right now. Otherwise, I would stay and chat."

"Wait," the Architect said. "I'm not supposed to do this, but I think I'd like a dance."

I took him back to the private dance room. "So, what do you mean you're not supposed to get a dance?" I took off my top and climbed onto his lap.

"Well, it was something I read that said you aren't supposed to get dances from girls you like."

"Oh no. Are you talking about the Mystery Method?" I asked.

"Oh, wow. You've heard of it. I guess that's not going to work, then…"

This was well before Mystery, the pickup-artist creator of the Mystery Method, was doing a competitive reality show on MTV. Not many people had heard of it at that time, and I only happened to be aware of it because some women had posted about it on the stripper message boards. The Mystery Method was essentially a set of instructions on how to talk to women and get them to have sex with you. In pickup-artist circles, strippers and waitresses were considered "hired guns," and they are supposed to be harder to pick up. If a guy could pick up one of us, they'd get extra cool-guy points amongst their douchey pickup-artist friends. Essentially, the approach they claimed worked best was to say mildly insulting things, called "negs," and then not pay them anything so they wouldn't see the guy as a customer. In fact, ideally, a guy was supposed to pretend he was friends with the DJ and then try to get the stripper to pay him to give her a lap dance. I couldn't imagine something like that working in a million years, even with the most gullible strippers I knew.

I initially thought, *Oh no, he's one of them.* I had been waiting to meet one of those guys in the club, just so I could shoot him down because I found their overconfidence obnoxious, especially their stance of not tipping or buying any dances. I continued to ask the Architect about his understanding of the Mystery Method, and he told me about a book he had read called, *The Game: Penetrating the Secret Society of Pickup*

Artists by music journalist Neil Strauss. The Architect claimed that it had increased his confidence and that he felt a lot more comfortable talking to women after having read it.

"And it told you not to get dances from strippers, huh?"

"Yeah. I guess I broke that rule. But you were going to go off and give dances to someone else if I didn't get you back here."

The more I talked to the Architect, the less he seemed like a manipulative pickup-artist type. We did ten dances and he told me about his summer travels in the Netherlands and Italy. He talked about how he had gotten to meet distant family members who lived in small mountain villages in Italy and what an exciting experience that had been for him.

Our dances ended when DJ Russ announced the last song of the night. The Architect pulled out his money and handed it to me along with the same business card he had given me the last time. I gave him my dancer email and told him to have a good night.

When I got to the dressing room, I discovered that he had given me $200 for the ten dances which would have been right on a regular night, but since it was discount dance night, he should have only given me $100. I wasn't sure if he had done that on purpose or if he hadn't realized it was discount dance night. Regardless, I was much more impressed by him than I would have been if he had just told me he didn't get dances and was only at the club because he was friends with the DJ.

The next day I worked at the library, and when it wasn't busy, I searched to see if we had *The Game*. I had been intrigued by the Architect's claim that the book was more an inspiration for his confidence than a manual for how to trick women into sleeping with him. I took it home that night and began speeding through it. Neil Strauss had entered the world of pickup artists as an outsider looking to improve his own success with women. Along the way, he ran into a lot of very douchey guys who were all about trying to out-pickup each other as though it were a competitive sport. I didn't like the way many of them no longer saw the women as people but rather conquests to use for the purpose of bragging to their friends. Arguably, many of my customers probably did not see me as a person, but it was different because I had volunteered to be their temporary sex object. No one was manipulating me, and I was making my own decisions. Overall, I had mixed feelings about the narrator. On one hand, I wanted him to get over his feelings of awkwardness and succeed at learning how to talk to women confidently, but on the other, I watched him transform into this competitive pickup artist who started hooking up with women left and right just to see if he could do it. He got completely wrapped up in picking up women, but at least he maintained the self-awareness that he was getting too consumed by living the life of a top pickup artist and eventually realized that lifestyle was not going to help him meet someone he really connected with. In the end, the book became something of a cautionary tale about getting too ingrained in the seduction subculture.

I realized, as I was reading it, that I wanted to discuss the book with the Architect. I also felt a little guilty for him overpaying me by $200 for his dances, especially considering the fact that he thought the girls who worked at Henry's liked to rip people off. I wasn't exactly sure what I wanted, but I figured at the very least the Architect would be a good regular to cultivate. I emailed him, inviting him to come see me at Henry's sometime and get a free dance. I told him I wanted to make up for how much he had overpaid me the last time and prove that not all of Henry's girls ripped people off.

The Architect replied that he hadn't known that he'd overpaid and he appreciated my honesty. He said he would try to stop in and see me, and a few days later, he did. I gave him his free dance and he bought several more. I expected him to ask me out again and this time

I realized I was waiting for it. When he asked, I said yes. I even whispered to him my real name and gave him my phone number. We made plans to meet at a nice Italian restaurant in Ann Arbor for drinks.

I'd never planned to date a customer and I was surprised that I was willing to. At the same time, though, I hadn't actually dated anyone in almost a year, and the only kind of place where I ever met anyone anymore was in a strip club. I finally figured that, in the worst-case scenario, I could just decide not to see him again. He had said he didn't like coming into Henry's anyway, so I knew I wouldn't have to worry about any fallout there.

I realized the one major advantage to dating a customer was that he already knew what I did for a living. If I were to meet someone in my regular everyday life, I would have to deal with telling that person that I was a stripper and hoping that they would somehow be okay with it. That was one of the many reasons I had previously decided not to even bother dating anyone while I was still stripping. But it was beginning to look as though I was going to be stripping in a long-term way, and it was unrealistic to not date at all for those years.

In popular culture, when the topic of dating strippers came up, many people took the line that it would be gross to be with such a loose woman with no morals. Either that, or they thought it would give them some type of status with other men, such as the wannabe pickup artists. So, my greatest fear was that if I saw someone outside the club, he would have trouble separating the fantasy from the reality and not be able to see me as a real person. All of my conversations with the Architect thus far seemed to indicate that he wouldn't treat me that way, but it was still too early to know that for sure.

On the night of our date, I made a point of dressing as normally as possible. I wore a pencil skirt, an unrevealing blouse, and flats. I did put on light makeup but nothing in the ballpark of what Penelope would wear, and I also wore my glasses. I proceeded cautiously and did not expect much. In a way, I saw going out on a date with the

Architect as a social experiment, as I often considered my life experiences when I was unsure of what I was doing.

The Architect talked a lot, which was good for me. We quickly found out we were on the same page politically and agreed about a lot of pop-culture phenomena as well. I also found out that he was about to turn thirty-six, which was older than anyone I had dated before. He was a full ten years older than me, but somehow the fact that he was born in 1970 instead of 1969 made that okay. It still felt fine to date someone born in the '70s. Anything before that would have seemed too old, considering that I had been born in 1981.

I ordered a full meal because I hadn't eaten anything yet that day. I let the Architect pay, but I determined that if this was going to continue, I would pay for the next meal. I was definitely not interested in him as a sugar daddy, nor did I want him to think I wanted that.

At that point, I felt safe with him and I agreed to go back to his place when he invited me. The pretense was to play pool in his basement, which he claimed was more original than watching a movie. We talked all night, during which I drank way too much wine and ended up puking in his toilet. At the time, I didn't consider that a weird thing to do on a date, so I wasn't embarrassed. After he gave me an unwrapped toothbrush he had lying around, we made out and I fell asleep.

The next morning, I went back to my apartment to recover from my terrible hangover and get some more sleep. He called me later that day and asked if I wanted to come over to recuperate together. He knew he was violating some major dating rule by calling me the next day, but he didn't care. I went over because I knew I wouldn't be working that night with my head feeling the way it did.

The Architect came on strong. He often initiated advancements in our relationship much earlier than I had ever been comfortable with before. After just a week or two of dating, I told him my sister was engaged, and he began to make subtle engagement jokes with me. I would laugh with obvious nervousness, and he would get the hint and back off.

One of the kinks we had to work out in the beginning of our relationship was how he described me to other people. I quickly had to make sure that he did not tell anyone I might eventually meet that I was a stripper. The Architect was an extremely honest person and had trouble replicating the white lies that kept my job as a stripper a secret. Although he could tell people I was a librarian, if a situation came up wherein we had to explain why I was working at night, he would just tell people I also worked in a bar. I tried to get him to just say "waitress" instead, but the lie went against his code of ethics.

That became a bigger issue when people would ask us how we met. To this day, I really can't remember who I told what regarding that inevitable question. Some people thought we met where I was waitressing—though the name of the restaurant in those stories has unfortunately varied a little too much—and others that we met at a coffee shop. In retrospect, it really would have made the most sense to just tell people we met through an online dating site, which would have required no further explanations. Despite having few taboos about anything sexual, I still considered online dating as something that just seemed too wild for me to do in 2005, so I didn't consider that a viable explanation at the time.

17

The Architect wasn't technically the first customer I had agreed to go on a date with. I had previously allowed another customer, when I was still relatively new at Bogart's, to break me down to the point of agreeing to meet up with him at a restaurant. I had been drinking more than usual and the customer, Charles, who was about twenty years older than me, just kept saying emotionally manipulative things that made me feel as if I couldn't say no. He kept implying that I was somehow an insincere person if I didn't agree to go out with him. I continued saying no, and he kept saying it would just be a free dinner and, "How could that hurt anything?" I should have just gotten up and walked away at that point, but I let him keep pushing me and finally said I would meet him.

The next day, I woke up feeling ill about the situation. I didn't want to be a liar, but I really did not want to meet that man. I always had been good about doing things I promised to do, even if I really didn't want to do them anymore. I felt obligated at that point, but ultimately, I decided not to do it. He had made me feel responsible to him, and that didn't make any sense. I decided to assume that he would also realize, in his sobriety, that making plans with a stripper had been a bad idea.

By the time I started working at Henry's, I had stopped worrying about seeing him again and eventually forgot about him. Then one day several months later, he came into Henry's. I had come out of the dressing room and there he was, sitting at a table, looking at me expectantly. I decided to just avoid him and not make eye contact. I didn't want to engage with that guy again and I didn't feel like finding out whether he had showed up for our date or not.

At first, avoidance was effective. He had plenty of girls going up to him, trying to hustle dances, and he seemed happy with the attention. Then, on the last song of my second stage set, just as my anxiety about him being in the building had gone down, he came up to my stage to tip me. I smiled awkwardly and he asked me to come over to his table.

It was funny how money added a sense of obligation sometimes. I went over, and he asked me why I hadn't shown up to the date. I told him I figured we were both drunk, so he wouldn't remember. I acted like a flighty stripper. He tried to guilt me, so I apologized again and told him I had to get to a customer who was waiting for me.

I walked away, but then he came back a little while later, asking to buy me a drink. I asked him if he was going to keep complaining about how I stood him up, and he said no, so I agreed to sit with him again. We ended up hanging out for a while and he bought a bunch of dances from me. As soon as they were over, he began trying to get me to make plans with him again. This time, I gave him a definitive no and told him I had a boyfriend.

Then he started his whole guilt-trip line. "Oh, you don't really care about me. You just want my money."

At that point, I realized this guy was setting up and creating his own disappointments. He had chosen to come into a strip club and talk to strippers and buy dances. There was nothing about that type of transaction to suggest that I was leading anyone on, considering that it was obviously my job. I knew plenty of girls who actively led customers on, but at worst, I just tried to not straight-out reject them so I wouldn't hurt their feelings.

Sometimes I had to be very blunt with customers or they wouldn't get it. Another customer I continually said no to, who kept pursuing me anyway, was a short, squat fifty-year-old man named Howie. He told me he worked as a photographer for ten dollars an hour. He talked a lot and was convinced that he knew a lot about just about everything. It was usually easy to talk to him, because all I had to do was randomly interject a relevant question, and he would continue to babble about whatever it was that he thought was important.

One time, he told me that his main job was to take pictures in some guy's massive private library. At first, I thought he was lying because he thought it would impress me as a librarian. Then later, he offered to try to get me a job with his boss, helping categorize and organize his collection.

Unlike some previous customers, I knew Howie was not doing the white knight thing. He was pursuing the fantasy of seeing me in my real life that would create an opportunity for us to be together. I asked him what he thought his employer would pay per hour and when he told me, I pointed out that I was used to making a lot more. I realized with Howie that it was best to be as direct as possible. I also asked him how he expected to explain to his employer how he met me, and he did not have a good answer for that.

Howie was a little too wrapped up in his own fantasies and not very grounded in reality. One time, he told me that he had gone to the grand opening for a new Ikea in our area and that a beautiful woman in the family that owned the company was standing near the entrance, giving out cookies. He described her as his ideal woman, rich and gorgeous, and then asked me why he couldn't be with a woman like her.

Howie also asked me to meet him at a restaurant, but at that point, he finally understood we were never going to see each other romantically. He offered me one hundred dollars to have dinner with him and secretly wear a remote-control vibrator toy in my underwear that he could activate at will throughout the meal. I told him that was too little money, and he complained that he would also have to buy the toy and the dinner, so he shouldn't have to pay more than that. I had to point out to him that one hundred dollars wasn't worth my time, since I would have to meet him out on a night I could be working and making much more money than that.

About a year later, I saw Howie at a movie theater, rambling to the young woman behind the ticket counter. I could already tell by the body language of the girl that she was annoyed and hoped he would go away. I quickly turned in the other direction and had the Architect go up and buy our tickets, so I did not have to worry about him seeing and recognizing me.

I learned a lot about how to deal with or just avoid difficult customers. During the beginning of one evening shift, I had started a conversation with a guy who only wanted to talk about pills. He kept talking about how great he thought Xanax was and then offered me some. I declined, but he persisted in telling me all about how I was missing out. It was a little like one of those scenarios people warned us about when I was a kid, about how someone was going to try to push drugs on us and make us feel uncool about saying no. I tried changing the topic of conversation to lap dances, and he indicated that he might be more interested in one if I took one of his pills. Before I could leave on my own accord, I got called to the stage. He tried to stop me with an offer to watch my drink.

"Why would I need you to watch my drink? I can bring it to the stage with me."

"But that would let me know you were planning on coming back," he slurred.

"But I'm not coming back."

He acted genuinely hurt. "But don't you trust me?" It was ridiculous how obvious he was being, though his exact plan wasn't clear. It was unlikely that he could successfully drug me and get me to leave the bar with him in a semiconscious state while the bouncers just stood there. Maybe his plan had been to get me so pliant that I wouldn't care if he molested me during a lap dance. Either way, on my way to the stage, I told Nick and one of the other girls and asked them to spread the word to be careful around him.

Sometimes customers made up obvious lies to try to impress me. Probably the most ridiculous was a young guy who kept insisting he was a very important music producer and promoter. He kept trying to guess what bands I liked, presumably to then tell me he had something to do with producing their music. I told him I mostly only listened to noise music—not true, but funny. He decided, based on my age, that the most important band he could impress me with was Nirvana. He claimed that he had been instrumental in helping them to become famous. I asked him how old he was. He must have realized he had made a mistake, because he refused to tell me his age. According to my estimate, this guy was a few years older than me at the most, which would have made him twenty-eight. That would have made him sixteen when Kurt Cobain died, which meant he had helped make them famous when he was eleven or twelve.

Just as my customers tried to bullshit me, I had plenty who assumed I was trying to bullshit them. It wasn't unusual for them not to believe that I had graduated from the University of Michigan. I could tell by the look on their faces. Most of those who suspected that I was lying did not bother pursuing the truth further, because they either didn't care or just assumed most strippers made up stuff about themselves anyway. One time, a guy a little older than me who was in the architecture graduate program at Michigan said, "Yeah, sure you did," and rolled his eyes at me. For some reason, I could not let that go, so I stayed and talked to him. I could deal with people thinking I was a slut because I was a stripper or any of the other stigmas that went with the job, but my ego got extra riled up if someone implied that I must also be stupid and incapable of graduate level study.

He began asking me questions and I told him all about my program at the School of Information. We even exchanged SAT scores, which I normally avoided. There wasn't a way to say I'd scored in the ninety-ninth percentile without people thinking I was bragging. I didn't care at that point, though, because I had apparently enrolled myself in a stupid prove-yourself-to-this-random-guy contest, and I might as well pull out the big guns. The guy, though, just gave me another, "You're full of shit" look. Apparently, people didn't think they could get a lap dance from someone who had done better than them on a standardized test. Those tests only measured verbal and logical intelligences and in practice only functioned as gauges of how good a person was at doing schoolwork, as opposed to greater indicators of life success such as emotional intelligence—which I probably I would have scored pretty poorly on at the time.

Since he was firing questions at me, I decided to turn the tables and throw the burden of proof on him. I decided to force him to prove that he was who he said he was. As I asked him more about himself, I found out that he had majored in philosophy as an undergrad, also at Michigan. I mentioned that I had taken a philosophy class as one of my cognates—we could take two classes in pretty much any field outside the SI curriculum—and I described the class and named the professor. His eyes brightened. "Wait, you had a class with him?"

"Yeah. I loved how he would get chalk all over his hands and then absentmindedly rub them on his shirt and head when he got excited. He'd walk around with chalk all over his body and just not give a fuck."

"Yeah, I remember that. He did that in the class I took with him too." He paused. That was something only a student who had actually taken one of this man's classes would know. "Okay, I believe you. Why are you here, then? That just doesn't make sense!"

I shrugged. "Bad decisions, I guess. Want a lap dance?"

After giving the guy five dances, I stopped back by his table and asked, "So why are *you* here, then?" He told me all about how he was engaged to be married soon and how he knew it was a big mistake. I asked him if he had knocked up his fiancée or something. He said no, so I asked why he didn't just call off the wedding if he was unhappy. It turned out that her family was very rich and he didn't want to lose the money he would soon be marrying into.

"So, you're going to choose money over love and happiness?" I asked him.

"Yeah." He gulped. "I guess I am."

For a long time, I worried I would see a customer come into Henry's whom I had also seen at the library, or vice-versa. My theoretical plan to deal with that situation was just to play dumb and not acknowledge that I knew the person from the other venue. A few customers did try to ask me a bunch of questions about what library I worked at, and I would never give them any information. One even told me he was going to go wander around area libraries until he found me. I suspected that he would probably lose interest in this endeavor by the next day, but it still made me nervous.

I finally had my first crossover with a man named Vincent, who came into the library looking for Al Franken's *The Truth (With Jokes)*. The book was still due to be released, so I wasn't able to get it for him. I offered to put him on the waiting list, but a few people were already ahead of him. He said that was okay, because he would probably just go out and buy it himself once it was released. We then began to talk about Al Franken's last popular book, *Lies: And the Lying Liars Who Tell Them*, and in the middle of that discussion, I realized why he looked familiar. My first thought had been that he must have been in the library before, but then I recognized him as someone who had come into Henry's.

The encounter had been a few months before and he had been in with a group of friends, one of whom had come up to me to tell me about Vincent. He was a widower. His wife had died from a terminal illness about a year earlier and they had taken him out to have some fun. The friend wanted to pay me to give the guy as many lap dances as he wanted. Vincent did not look older than forty, so it was obvious his wife had died way too young.

He had looked like a guy who was trying to have fun, but he had a definite sadness about him. Or maybe I only noticed it because I knew about his tragic history. I remembered it being hard to get fully into the lap dance mindset, because I suspected that lap dances weren't really going to help him with his sorrow, even though I knew his friend meant well.

As he stood in front of me in the library, I immediately began to fear that he would recognize me. Luckily, someone else came up to the desk behind him and I moved on to attend to that person's question. There was still nothing to indicate that he knew who I was, so I breathed a sigh of relief and considered that I might have just dodged a bullet.

Then a few weeks later, he came back into Henry's. He was sitting at the bar with some friends and I was just sure he would recognize me, especially since he had been in the library so recently. We couldn't really hide for long when working in a strip club though, because we'd eventually get called up onstage. As I did my set, I would periodically look over at him to see if he was looking at me, but he seemed more involved in the conversation he was having with his friends. I knew I looked pretty different as Penelope, but it was hard for me to objectively gauge just how different I looked.

A little while later, as I was walking past the bar, one of Vincent's friends stopped me and asked me to join them. I hesitated for a moment, but I was curious about how long I could continue to get away with this guy not recognizing me. As we all chatted, Vincent ended up talking more to me and his friend went away to get some dances with another girl. He bought me a beer and we discussed politics for a while, finding out we had a good amount in common. I gave him some dances and then went back to the bar with him to hang out some more. It was pretty obvious at that point that he was not going to figure out who I was even though we had actually had a similar conversation that included Al Franken just a few weeks ago at the library.

Then Vincent began to talk about his wife's death and how it had been such a surprise to them when they found out she was sick. "I haven't felt ready till now to actually go out with someone. I feel like you're someone I can really talk to. Do you think you'd like to go get a coffee or something with me sometime?"

I replied, "I'm so sorry—I have a boyfriend."

It felt awful to crush a guy who had gone through something like that, especially on his first attempt to put himself out there. I was usually annoyed by guys who assumed that my attention meant I wanted to see them outside of the club. With Vincent, though, I completely understood. I had gotten along with him a lot more easily than I often did with my customers. Even if I'd been single, I might not have said yes. I might not have been able to handle the pressure of following in a beloved wife's footsteps.

He seemed to take it well, or at least did not want to make me feel bad about saying no to him. I wanted to offer him something, so I suddenly found myself saying, "You know we've met before?"

"You mean here?"

"Well, yes. But somewhere else too."

He stared at me blankly. I could still back out of this if I wanted to, but apparently, I was ready to just go ahead and open the full can of worms. In a way, I was testing my own boundaries, trying to see what exactly would happen if I removed the separation between my two lives.

"We talked about Al Franken before. You were looking for his newest book."

Then I could see the light bulb go off. "Wait, that was you?" he asked me, dumbfounded.

"Shhhh!" I said, putting my finger to my lips. "It's a secret. No one here knows…"

Although a lot of the women I worked with did know my real first name, I hadn't actually told any of them what library I worked at.

"Wow. For real?"

I then told him my story and made him swear to secrecy. I gave him a few more dances and walked away, hoping I hadn't made a terrible mistake. He seemed like an honest person and I hoped I could trust him.

Some of my most interesting adventures were actually with female customers. We did not get a lot of them, but I was always more than happy to entertain them when we did. As per the rules of Henry's, and many other strip clubs for that matter, female customers were only allowed in the club in the company of a man, to ensure that they weren't prostitutes looking for johns. I had tried asking the bouncers about lesbians who might want to come in but never really got a straight answer—they were sticking to their policy. If a woman came in, she was usually with her boyfriend or husband.

If a couple came into the club, I found it was important to examine the body language of the woman before I considered approaching them. Sometimes the woman gave off nothing but a look of being uncomfortable—it was obvious that her partner had dragged her to the club and she really didn't want to be there. There was really no point in even trying to engage those couples. I didn't want to go give a dance to a guy whose wife was right there and had a scowl on her face. The fantasy of watching his wife get a dance was usually his own, and she was only going along with it to placate him. I didn't want to give a dance to a reluctant party. It didn't seem right to be touching someone who clearly didn't want to be touched.

When a woman was looking around and giving indications of enjoying herself, such as smiling at the stage and tipping, that was another story. I wasn't the only one who liked those kinds of couples. I often didn't see them soon enough and another girl would swoop in and be their fun for the night.

Dancing for couples was pretty easy. I could usually get away with charging them extra per dance since I was dancing for two people. Then I could direct most of my attention on the woman while the man sat there watching. It was a win-win for everyone.

I gave several dances one night to a couple and began sliding my hand under the shirt of the woman. I asked her if it was okay and she told me to continue. As I reached her breasts, I discovered that they were implants. She did not seem like the type to get breast implants. I had always associated breast augmentation with women who were especially fixated on how they looked or who worked in the sexual-entertainment industry. She didn't fit either of those types. As my hand progressed farther upward, I realized she had no nipples. Fortunately, I fully contained my surprise. It took me a minute to realize she was a breast cancer survivor. I hadn't before considered that as a reason that a woman might want breast implants. I couldn't imagine how it would feel to have breasts removed. It made total sense that women might want to replace them with something.

Apparently, I had done a good job of containing my surprise, because they tipped me well and the woman beamed at me. When she visited the ladies' room, her husband mentioned to me that she had "gone through some difficult times" but that he was happy she was able to go out and have fun again.

On the other hand, women could be very aggressive, which I didn't really expect at first. My guard was often down with women, which made it easy for things to go too far. I gave several dances one night to a young woman who kept getting her male friend to buy her more dances with me. It was easy to push away the roaming hands of men, but I had trouble pushing away her hands. She assumed she could put them wherever she wanted and I didn't stop her. Maybe I didn't know how to stop her, or maybe I didn't want to. I left that whole situation feeling ambivalent.

18

I originally had no intention of staying in Michigan. For the longest time, I would comfort myself with the knowledge that I could move back to the Chicago area when I graduated. I had also taken a little break from applying for jobs, and I had to admit that was due to my new relationship with the Architect. I wasn't sure where I wanted to be, so I didn't choose one direction or another. The lease for my apartment would soon be up at the end of August, which meant that I had to start making decisions.

I needed to see what would happen with the Architect. I had never had a relationship that had started so quickly and also seemed very healthy. There were no games, and he openly communicated how he felt about me. I was learning how to communicate my feelings in an honest way, which I had always had trouble with before.

One night, the possibility of moving in with the Architect came up. He said, "It would be too early for us to live together. That would be crazy, right?" But, I thought he might be feeling out how open I was to the idea. We had only been dating for a month and a half, and although I had good feelings about our future, I wasn't ready for that type of commitment. Since Aurora and my lease was almost up, she was getting ready to move. She was finishing her final semester at Wayne State that summer and was planning on moving to the UK to be with her fiancé, Brian. I began looking around for apartments that didn't require me to sign a lease for an entire year. I found one I liked in Ypsilanti, the biggest city next to Ann Arbor, which would allow me to cancel my lease with a month's notice and a penalty charge. The apartment had two bedrooms, so I started seeking out a female roommate online.

I had a hard time admitting to myself that I was staying in Michigan for a man, because I never thought I would do something like that. I had a harder time admitting that to the Architect. When I did, he was delighted. Originally, I came up with some type of excuse about wanting to continue to strip in a place far from my hometown friends and family.

Before Aurora left, I decided it would be fun to throw her a bachelorette party, which was also the perfect opportunity for us to go to Danny's, an all-male strip club. I was really curious to see what it would be like on the other side of the stage, so to speak.

Only one of Aurora's other Michigan friends was available since the plan was so last minute. After stopping for dinner, we drove to Windsor, Canada, where Danny's was located. I had gotten Aurora plenty of bachelorette-party paraphernalia, including a penis headband, which she was happy to wear.

As we got through the line to pay and enter the club, I was surprised to see a sign about how absolutely no male customers were allowed in the building. I was sure their reasons differed from why clubs with women dancers didn't allow other unaccompanied women. It was unlikely they were worried about male prostitutes coming in to solicit. They might have been concerned about men getting jealous and possibly violent toward the dancers, if they saw their girlfriends or wives getting excited. I also suspected that their reasoning was motivated by homophobia as well. They didn't want gay men in the club enjoying the show, where potentially homophobic female customers could claim to feel uncomfortable and take offense. That was all the more ridiculous because it was obvious that some of the dancers there were gay.

When we entered the main floor of the club, I could see that the majority of Danny's customers were in bachelorette parties like ours. Unlike the lethargic men who came into Henry's, these women were wildly enthusiastic. They were hooting and hollering at the stage, and there was laughter everywhere. This was the first time I'd seen a strip club that actually reminded me of how they were represented in the movies. The male dancers were significantly more theatrical with their stage sets as well, which made sense because they had more incentive to perform spiritedly with an enthusiastic audience.

Most of them did themed sets, and it became obvious pretty quickly that this club did full nude. There was a fireman with his hose, a police officer with handcuffs, and an Uncle Sam with his patriotic top hat. The weirdest set by far, though, was a guy who used a bathtub. The tub, which had a hole in the front, was brought out to the middle of the stage. As he did his performance, it became clear why the tub had the hole in the front. I thought it was funny to watch a man fuck a bathtub, but the crowd seemed to find it exciting. Upon closer observation, I saw that a lot of these guys were using cock rings—and probably Viagra—to keep a hard show for a good portion of their performances.

We were given a small table to the side of the stage and we spent a lot of time watching the behavior of the women in the club. Our little bachelorette party was tame by comparison. We probably did not drink nearly as much as some of the others, but that couldn't be the only thing explaining their outrageous behavior. Many women felt free to just reach out and grab whatever body parts they wanted as the strippers walked by. They felt they were completely entitled to touch these men without asking. I watched one guy try to walk through the crowd and a group of women wouldn't let him go. He kept gesturing that he was going somewhere, but they kept reaching out and touching him as though they were completely free to do whatever they wanted to his body. I felt uncomfortable for him. That kind of behavior would not have been openly tolerated at Henry's. I was surprised to find myself thinking my customers were actually well-behaved by comparison.

But then again, it might have been a matter of people taking things as far as they could get away with. The bachelorette party is a weird cultural tradition. There seemed to be an underlying assumption that you could do whatever you wanted at one of these events and then go back to acting like a normal person with self-control the next day.

I asked Aurora if she would like to get a lap dance and she said she would. I kept asking her who she was interested in among the guys we saw walking around the club, but she kept shrugging. She said that most of them were too muscular for her taste. I asked her what kind of guy she would be interested in, and she said her ideal dancer would be Jewish-looking and skinny. I scoured the club to find the guy who was closest to fitting that description. A lot of these guys were busy, so I might have to go seek one out instead of waiting for one to come to our table. These men probably didn't have to hustle much to have a good night. It looked like it was easy for them to get dance after dance.

Finally, I found a stripper with a slightly darker complexion—he probably had some Italian ancestry—who was less bulky than the other guys in the club. I wouldn't have called him scrawny by any normal guy metrics, but by male-stripper standards, he wasn't very muscular. I pointed him out to Aurora and asked if she liked him and she said yes. I wandered over to him and pointed out my table, asking him to stop by when he got a chance.

He took his time coming over and, in the meantime, we examined the placard on our table that explained the different types of dances available. There were pedestal dances for twenty dollars and private dances for thirty dollars a song. A stripper finally came by our table and said hi. He was a short, enthusiastic, Hawaiian-looking guy. I asked him about the difference between the dances. He explained that the pedestal dances were performed on a stool right in front of the customer and the private dances were done in the back. I looked behind me, not having realized there was a whole dance area there. I could see that there were couches but could only see the heads of the women getting private dances with the guys gyrating on top of them.

When Aurora's stripper came to our table, I asked Aurora what she wanted, and she said she thought she could probably only handle a pedestal dance. He put a little block in front of her and leaned his head into the side of her face. Then he pulled back and began manually working on his erection, which he seemed to be having a little trouble with. I wasn't sure why he felt he had to maintain it during the dance and began to feel a little awkward for him. I guess it was part of the presentation. I was glad that was something I didn't have to worry about. I couldn't imagine having to get aroused on command and especially for the sake of performance.

Once Aurora's dance was over, he asked her if she would like another and she said no, as she fought to catch her breath. I paid him and gave him a tip. When I turned back to her, she was still doubled over, laughing. She said she was way too sensitive. He had blown air into her ear, and that was apparently enough to really do her over. I was glad she'd enjoyed her dance, despite the weird dick stuff he had been doing.

I wanted to get the full male-strip-club experience, so I needed to get a dance as well. I also decided to get a pedestal dance. I couldn't see what was going on over in the private dance area very well, but I could tell it was going to be more contact than I really wanted, especially considering how much I already saw happening out on the floor during pedestal dances--including what basically amounted to hand jobs. I had tried to wander back to the private area just because I was nosy and wanted to see exactly what was going on, but a guy looked up at me during his dance in such a way as to suggest I'd better wander back. It looked like he was trying to get his customer off.

I decided to ask the Hawaiian-looking guy because I thought he deserved my business the most. He was walking around and smiling, unlike a lot of the men in the club. He had also been the only guy to stop at our table and talk to us. He ended up being even more enthusiastic than Aurora's stripper. He was less about bringing his dick out and more about getting on top of me, including licking my ear. Like Aurora, I was pretty sure one dance was enough for me.

We ended our big international jaunt by getting a bizarre lecture from the American border control officer manning the entrance back into the US from Canada. I had brought my passport, but Aurora and her friend only had their driver's licenses with them. This was before they were officially enforcing the Enhanced Driver's License requirement at the Canadian border but were in the process of warning people that it would soon be the official proof of citizenship required to get back into the United States.

The border patrol officer was a short man with a patchy mustache. He asked us why we had gone to Canada, and I told him we had been to some bars.

"Which bars?" he asked, clearly not approving of my nonspecific answer.

"Danny's."

I braced myself for a reaction to this, but he had none. After examining my passport, he handed it back.

"See, this woman is smart. She has a passport. I can verify that she is an American citizen who belongs in this country." He pointed at me. That was probably the worst compliment I'd ever received, which was saying a lot from a stripper.

He continued to hold the other IDs, trying to stare ominously. "You think this proves you are a US citizen?" he asked my friends.

They nodded uncertainly.

"You know Arnold Schwarzenegger?"

We all nodded, beginning to suspect this was going to turn into a joke.

"Well, he has a California license. Yes, that's right—you can get a license when you aren't born here. He was born in Austria and can never be president of the United States. But you would never know that looking at his California state-issued license. That's why these IDs don't tell me anything about you. I have no way to know you are who you say you are. You could be anyone from anywhere trying to get into this country and do harm to her citizens." He paused. "You know they give Michigan driver's licenses to people from Iraq?"

We tried to make serious faces as though what he was saying was really important, and I resisted pointing out that Arnold Schwarzenegger was a US citizen—he couldn't have run for Governor of California otherwise—so he was a terrible example of someone whose state ID did not represent their legal identity. I was pretty sure this guy would have gone completely ballistic and detained us if I did anything to contradict him.

He continued to lecture my friends about bringing proper identification with them if they ever left the United States again and then threatened that he might not let them back into the country in the future unless they got enhanced drivers' licenses.

We realized that time-consuming power-tripping lectures like that were the reason the line to the American border had been so much longer than the polite, easygoing line at the Canadian border. After he finally let us pass the border and we took a moment to process what we had just heard, we couldn't stop laughing the rest of the way home.

Not long after that, I decided to make an investment in my success as a stripper. On the stripper message boards, a lot of girls talked about a seminar program they had attended that was supposed to help with their lap dance sales skills. There was online material for sale as well as a day-long seminar that was held regularly in Las Vegas. A lot of them swore by the in-person seminar and reported seeing a subsequent spike in their earnings after attending it. As I was beginning to see myself as a professional stripper, it seemed like a good step for my future, plus I'd always wanted to visit Vegas.

I brought the idea up with the Architect, and he encouraged me to do it, offering to come along so we could turn the whole trip into a minivacation. We decided to go for four nights and divide the cost between us. I bought the airline tickets, and he bought the hotel room. This was the first time I had ever taken a vacation with someone I was dating and, when I thought about it, the first time I had planned a real vacation as an adult. Every trip I'd taken previously had either been just a short road trip or to visit friends.

The Architect picked the Mirage for us to stay at. I had encouraged him to find a cheaper hotel when we were looking at what was available online, but he insisted we needed to be on the strip in order to get the full Vegas experience. We planned the trip so that we could do whatever we wanted on the first three days, and then I would go to my seminar on the last day before we came back home.

We started drinking pretty early every day but managed to at least pace ourselves with our steady stream of piña coladas and all-you-can-eat buffets. That—combined with the time difference, which we never fully adjusted to—had us going to bed fairly early each night. We didn't stay up past midnight, which was probably not the way you were supposed to party in Vegas.

Previously, I had been indifferent to the idea of gambling. Mathematically, the odds really were stacked against you, but I wanted to get the full Vegas experience. I started at the nickel slot machines and managed to make forty dollars. Then the Architect wanted to visit the roulette table. At first, I insisted that I was only going to watch, but after a few rolls, I wanted to try putting some money down to see what would happen. I was still a cautious gambler, though. Choosing a number was clearly a quick way to lose money, so I began slowly putting my money down on red or black and eventually made $300. Then another night we stopped by the roulette table and I lost $100, which was a good reality check.

We also visited the famous Spearmint Rhino Gentlemen's Club. Many girls wrote online about their experiences working there and reported doing really well. I didn't feel ready to try a Vegas club, but I definitely wanted to at least check one out as a customer. We visited in the middle of the afternoon and it was not very busy. I was surprised by how incredibly dark it was. I knew the benefits of darker lighting in a strip club, but it was honestly hard to see the stage, which should have been the most well-lit part of the entire club. We got a few dances from a girl who stopped by to visit with us, and although she was probably pretty, it would have been hard to describe her afterward because it had been too dark to really make out her features. At least at this club, hustling skills might matter more than looks, because there was not a lot for a customer to distinguish between one girl and another when they could barely see them.

Our hotel had an adults-only pool lounge called Bare, which they did a good job of marketing to guests as a decadent experience where everyone was walking around naked. We paid extra to access it and I quickly decided I had no interest in taking my top off in broad daylight, especially when no one was paying me to do it. There were a few women who had no tops on, but all they got out of it, from what I could tell—besides no tan lines—was having Midwestern yokels gawk at them. The Architect and I just ended up drinking in an infinity pool and then having a swimming race with each other in the main pool, which I won. That must have significantly added to the sophisticated ambiance the Mirage was shooting for.

Throughout our trip, the Architect kept joking about how funny he thought it would be if we got drunk and married when we were in

Vegas. I kept saying that wasn't going to happen and then he continued to suggest we pretend we did anyway. His father had a history of playing practical jokes on people and the Architect thought it would be funny if we tricked him into thinking we got married in Vegas. As I had not met any of his family yet, I insisted that tricking his father into thinking we got married in Vegas would not be a very good way to introduce me to his family. Somehow, during all of that joking, we did end up buying a fake engagement ring and taking a few pictures with it. I said he could use the pictures to trick his friends, if he really wanted to, but not his family.

We did see a sign for the chapel at the Venetian and the Architect kept bringing it up and suggesting we visit it. I told him I was not drunk enough and he proceeded to keep ordering me drinks until I was ready. Eventually, I decided I would just go with him to "check it out." I later learned that most people who got married in Vegas had to stop by the smaller places on the outside of the strip. Those were the ones that were open twenty-four hours a day. The casino chapels tended to be more for scheduled weddings.

For years, the Architect says he would have married me right there, although I've always insisted that I wouldn't have gone through with it.

The stripper sales seminar was scheduled to be held at the Stratosphere. The only instructions I had were that we were to meet in the lobby. When I arrived, I discovered that the "lobby" pretty much blended in with the casino floor because there were multiple points of entry. After walking in circles, I eventually just waited in line to talk to the person at the front desk. When I asked the clerk if she knew where the stripper seminar was meeting, she just looked at me blankly and said she hadn't heard about anything like that happening that day.

I continued to walk in circles and then I saw a girl standing by herself, holding a handmade sign with the name of the seminar.

"Hi," I said cautiously as I walked up to her. "Where is everybody?"

"I just got here." She shrugged. "There are four or five people signed up."

I had thought this would be a bigger event. It was already five minutes past ten o'clock, when the seminar was supposed to start. But then again, strippers weren't typically morning people—or especially prompt, for that matter. As I stood around with her, two other girls showed up, and I began to feel a little self-conscious. I couldn't quite put my finger on what was making me feel uncomfortable, but that was one of the occasional consequences of being a functional introvert. I liked to enter new situations quietly and warm up on my own time. My plan had been to enter whatever room this seminar was being held in and just sit back quietly until I was ready to engage.

The other girls seemed to be bonding over some shared experiences and I was just standing there, trying not to look uncomfortable. Eventually, one more girl and our seminar leader, Bob, showed up. He said he had booked a suite for us. Bob was a middle-aged man in a business suit. From what I had gathered about him from his own contributions on the stripper message boards, he had been a pretty big strip club visitor, and through the friendships he made with the girls, he got interested in the sales side of the game and began suggesting techniques based on his own experiences in sales. Eventually, he began packaging his advice and selling it online and there were several strippers who swore by it on the message boards. The problem was that I usually felt weird around salesmen in general, probably because I was wary that they were going to try to sell me something.

We followed him up to the suite. He explained that another girl would probably be joining us—she had attended the seminar before and was coming back for a refresher. Refreshers were free for us once we'd attended the seminar the first time.

He had us go around the room and introduce ourselves, say where we were from, how long we'd been "dancing," and how much we averaged a night. Three of the other girls were from LA and one was from somewhere in the northwest. On my turn, I said I averaged $350 a night, which had actually been true in the month of June but had begun to go down in July. Bob said that was good for the Detroit area, which confirmed my suspicions that I could probably be making more money somewhere else.

There was practical advice about finding the right club to work in, basic club etiquette, and suggestions about apparel that was supposed to be more seductive than "slutty." A lot of the advice consisted of basic sales techniques, translated specifically to how they could be applied to selling lap dances, and self-improvement aphorisms such as, "Luck is where preparation meets opportunity."

Confidence was the most important factor in lap dance sales, followed by personality and sincerity, then attitude and overall looks. I doubted that this had been verified by any type of scientific method. I imagined that it was based on exit interviews of guys walking out of the private dance room. *Excuse me, sir. Will you take this short survey to tell us why you chose to get a dance with this stripper tonight? Thanks.* At the same time, though, I knew how important the confidence factor really was. I knew how my earnings could vary from one night to another based on my confidence. The trick, of course, was to figure out how to consistently maintain that confidence in the face of setbacks.

Bob advised us to never drink alcohol when we were on the clock because it was just a distraction. He also recommended that we act as though we were the hosts of the party. I wanted to point out that I didn't know how to act like that without alcohol, but I kept my hand down.

He brought up the Pareto Principal, which said, "Eighty percent of your sales come from twenty percent of your clients." The trick was to find the right customers. He advised us to learn what Rolexes looked like—I was pretty sure no one wore Rolexes in Henry's!—and become familiar with the differences in finer men's fabrics as far as suits and ties went so we could better identify men with more money to spend.

His sales advise was interesting and I could see how it would help if applied correctly. He pointed out that the best salesperson learned how to find the balance between building rapport—something women were typically better at—and closing a sale, which, he said, men were traditionally better at. He suggested we should try matching our customers' body language, which was a way to subconsciously create an emotional bond with them.

Bob also explained the basics of the "yes" close, which entailed asking a series of questions that the customer was likely to say yes to, such as, "There are some beautiful women in here tonight, aren't there?" and "You're having a good time tonight, aren't you?" We were supposed to ask at least five of these "yes" questions and then say something like, "Wouldn't you really enjoy getting a dance with me right now?" At that point, we would have successfully built up our "yes" ladders, and whoever we were talking to would be more inclined to say yes as a result.

At around this point, the girl joining us for a refresher finally arrived. She had been working the night before at a Vegas club and had been having such a good night that she had stayed into the morning because she had been on a roll, getting dance after dance.

He had her tell this crazy story about how she had managed to sell a VIP room to a man she had met at the airport. They had struck up a conversation and when she told him she was a stripper, he was interested. She had somehow gotten him to buy an hour with her alone in one of the airport's VIP lounges while he waited for his layover. Then our seminar leader pointed out that this might not always be the safest thing to do but that this particular girl was an überpro. Later, I wondered if she had been a plant to make some of the things we were learning seem attainable.

I managed not to act like a total wallflower during the workshop discussions, but I still participated less than the other girls. The seminar leader picked up on this and when I was asking for clarification on a point, he observed aloud that I seemed a little too reserved and kind of shy. I wasn't sure what kind of response I was supposed to give to that type of scrutiny. I probably should have acknowledged it and said it was something I was working on. I was aware of the problem and comments like that tended to undermine whatever confidence I did have, especially since I didn't like talking about it. Natural extroverts didn't understand how unhelpful it was to point that out, and I hadn't yet figured out how to own that part of myself.

He ended the seminar with the suggestion that if a girl really wanted to stand out in the club, she should look into adopting a unique skill set, like learning magic tricks or fire breathing. There was also practical advice about seeing oneself as a businessperson and declaring dance expenses for tax deductions. He emphasized that we should be saving and planning for retirement. We each received a seven-disc audio home-study set to use for further practice and review.

I left the seminar feeling unsure. I felt self-conscious about having my own lack of enthusiastic sales dynamism pointed out to me, but I also thought that using sales techniques in every interaction didn't really address the issue that many men wanted more than just a lap dance. Then again, I worked in metro Detroit, which was a high-mileage area compared to some others. Maybe it was easier to step around this in other cities, where there were not as many extras going on. The ultimate message of the seminar was that I needed to be more outgoing and work somewhere else.

I was interested in seeing someone do a yes-ladder to sell dances, though. I wasn't sure how well I could execute something like that myself. I had taken lots of notes, but I was bad at going back and looking at notes unless I had a pressing reason, such as an upcoming test. I also had trouble imagining myself privately rehearsing these types of conversations and was afraid that it would be obvious that I was applying a sales formula if I tried them with customers. That went back to the idea of building rapport, which I thought was something I did well but also wasted too much time doing. I wasn't very efficient with customers and wasted time not moving on quickly enough. At the same time, though, I didn't think I could build rapport if I acted like someone else. I hoped I would subconsciously internalize some of the ideas from the seminar and then just naturally execute them when the right time came.

19

Several months back, Aurora had mentioned that the colleague of one of her professors at Wayne State had done research on the information needs of prostitutes and was interested in looking at strippers next. I was intrigued but also a little scared. I asked her if she had told her professor about me and she said no, but she thought she'd ask me to see if I was interested. She thought this professor might want to talk to someone with a library science degree who actually worked as a stripper. I tentatively said she could tell her professor and he could talk to his colleague. If the woman wanted to contact me, Aurora could give her professor my Penelope email.

Not too long after that, I received an email from her. Her name was Dr. Anne Howard and she asked if I would be available to meet her for coffee sometime. She was willing to meet in Ann Arbor if it was more convenient for me. She wanted to tell me about her research and find out more about my experiences.

I refrained from giving her my real name at first and she did not seem to expect it. I tried to think of a way my identity could somehow be traced back through having Aurora as my roommate, but I couldn't really think of anything. I also figured there was no way for her to identify who I was just by meeting me in person. Then I supposed she could contact the School of Information and inquire about one of their students who might be a stripper and then describe me, but that seemed like a pretty ridiculous idea. I was also curious about her research, so I agreed to meet with her at a coffee shop in Ann Arbor that I rarely frequented.

I wasn't sure what to expect. I operated under the presumption that someone who was interested in sex workers would not harbor judgmental or disapproving feelings toward them. However, I wanted to confirm that by speaking with her before telling her more about myself. I also thought it would be problematic if she saw us as victims who needed saving because we weren't capable of making our own decisions and all of that kind of rhetoric.

Dr. Howard described herself and told me what her coat looked like so I could identify her when I arrived at the coffee shop. She had picked up on some of my hesitancy through our emails and did not even ask me what I looked like, which was pretty considerate on her part. She seemed to want to make sure I felt comfortable.

It turned out that Dr. Howard did not yet have a specific research agenda regarding strippers. She was interested in finding out what our information needs were, as we were a population that had not been considered for that type of research before, although she had yet to form a specific approach. She was still in the exploratory part of forming a research project; she kept using the term "exotic dancer" because she thought it was more respectful, which I had found many people liked to do. I was completely fine with being called a stripper, though, as that was the word preferred by most of the strippers I knew. I felt no need to sanitize what I was doing or try to make it sound more interesting.

Her previous research with street-level prostitutes had led to her involvement with a prostitution conference that was held every fall in Toledo, OH. From that, she had made contacts with others who were interested in similar research. She invited me to attend and come to some of the planning meetings with her.

I asked her more about the prostitution conference. What was the goal? Who attended it? She explained that most of the conference covered subjects related to street-level prostitution, and a lot of the people who attended were social workers who were trying to help women who were selling themselves because they were addicted to drugs. There were a few presentations on other topics related to sex work, and many women who were sex workers attended. I wasn't sure what to think, but decided that I liked Dr. Howard, so I agreed to go to one of their planning meetings with her.

Dr. Howard wanted to learn more about what stripping was like. I told her about the way the stage worked, hustling for dances, and how it varied from club to club. Since she wasn't sure how she would be conducting her research yet, she was also interested in ways to get girls to be research subjects for surveys and interviews. She saw me as a potential gateway to accessing them—I would be able to help her find subjects among my coworkers and at other clubs. I could go into dressing rooms and put up signs, offering gift cards for people to participate.

She said she had never been in a strip club and wanted to see what it was like. I explained the rule about having to have a male escort and she considered getting her husband to come into one with her but wasn't sure how comfortable he would be. Then I just went ahead and offered to take her to Henry's on a night I wasn't working. I just assumed the escort rule did not apply to me, because I already knew the bouncers who would have to enforce it.

I hadn't really stopped to think about what my coworkers would think about me coming into the club with her. I was more concerned with how at ease Dr. Howard would feel, but she seemed fine. We went and sat at a side stage and she continued to smile throughout the night and ask me questions. I told her stories about some of the girls she saw and what I knew about their lives. A bouncer and several girls came up to me to whisper in my ear and ask if she was my mom.

I looked around the club and realized some of the regulars had been looking at us too. They were probably making the same assumption. Why would I bring my mom to the strip club I worked at? Then again, there was the mother-daughter stripper duo that popped in on occasion, so anything really was possible in a strip club. I kept telling people that she was just my friend and she had wanted to see what Henry's was like.

Dr. Howard maintained a warm, approachable manner as we sat at the stage. We got drinks and I tipped the girls I was friendly with when they came up. Afterward, I asked her what she thought of the experience and she said it was fun and even better than she had thought it would be. Her work with street-level prostitutes had led her to believe that many women were either addicted to drugs or being coerced by someone else. Stripping obviously had those problems too, and there were all sorts of systemic factors that led women to do it, but I liked to think it wasn't as simple as that we were all just victims with no agency who needed someone to come in and save us. I could tell that Dr. Howard saw the difference. She had entered Henry's with an open mind and was interested in getting to know more "exotic dancers." She was probably hoping the visit would help her formulate the specifics of her research questions and the mechanism by which she would gather her data.

By the time of the prostitution conference, in early fall of that year, Dr. Howard had no specific plans about how she wanted to proceed and was beginning to think about changing the angle of her research. I was in no particular hurry and understood this was often the process of academic projects.

I went to the two-day conference with an open mind. I wasn't sure what to expect, but I ended up meeting a bunch of fascinating women. Dr. Howard introduced me to a woman with a master's degree in peace studies who had worked for years as a stripper around the world. She did a presentation on what it was like to be an exotic dancer. Her audience was a room full of women, most of whom were social workers. Her talk included a demonstration of a lap dance—done in a business suit—with an audience participant. I was aware of the tension between the providers and the sex workers in attendance, and she magically made it dissipate for a while. She had a warm and charismatic personality and it was easy to see how she would be a high earner at any club she went to. She was the kind of person who could talk to anyone and find a way to establish a connection. I was very impressed.

On the first night, I went out to dinner with her and a bunch of other women attending the conference. I gave an escort named Stacy a ride to the restaurant from the hotel where many of the conference attendees were staying. I realized, as I was talking to her, that I was interested in more than just the logistics of how she conducted her business. I had never said it aloud before to anyone else, but I was more than curious about prostitution. Plenty of customers had suggested it to me, and I realized that I was usually declining because either the price was not high enough or I wasn't sure how to do it safely and discreetly. I suspected that the customers who were willing to pay more were the ones who were waiting for me to name a price, and I didn't really know what that was yet.

I also knew that the step from stripping to prostitution was a big one from a social-taboo perspective. Being a stripper was still frowned upon, but it was considered more socially acceptable than being a prostitute. It also wasn't technically criminalized. There were many more people who would accept me as a stripper—or even better, an ex-stripper one day—than would accept me openly as a prostitute. As with my initial struggles with becoming a stripper, the biggest barrier for me in considering prostitution was the inevitable stigma and my own internalized whorephobia.

On the other hand, my own feelings about the stigma of prostitution had changed. I had definitely been one of those strippers who started out thinking I would never engage in sex acts for money.

But as it was, I was engaging in simulated sex and as far as I was concerned, I was already well versed in the girlfriend experience—kissing and pretending to like a customer as though you were his girlfriend—which many guys looked for in an escort. I had broken down and made out with a few customers when the price had been right and I didn't feel weird about it later. What I was doing wasn't really that far removed from sex, so why not just do it?

I was also attracted to what I considered the convenience factor of prostitution. There was no waiting around at a club for seven hours to find enough customers to pay you to entertain them. You either had business or you didn't. There was less hustling. If a customer was interested, they gave you a call and then it would be your job to give them a memorable experience so they would want to call you again. I imagined that, just like in the club, I could also specialize in customers interested in being dominated and market myself that way as well.

Prostitution also fit in with the most important parameter I had for sex work: I did not want to be photographed or filmed in any way. At the end of the day, I could still walk away whenever I felt like it and there would be no record of what I had done.

Finally, it made it much easier for me to envision seeing my student loans paid off in the near future. That was really the largest motivating factor. At that point, I had been stripping for about a year and had only managed to pay down about $8,000 of my outstanding $80,000 debt. I wasn't attacking it fast enough, and my interest rates were growing, particularly for my private loans.

Of course, the biggest negative that I had to consider was the fact that prostitution was completely illegal. If I got arrested, I would have a criminal record that would always be there and background checks would show I had been arrested for prostitution. That would absolutely kill my ability to ever enter a socially respectable career in a field like librarianship. It was also easy to imagine my face plastered on the Smoking Gun, which was a popular mid-aughts website that posted mug shots of sex workers.

At the same time, though, the kinds of lap dances we gave at Henry's and all the other clubs in the area technically could be considered acts of prostitution by the legal definition, according to Michigan law. All lap dances were supposed to be given three feet away from the customer and anything closer was considered prostitution. Of course, no customer anywhere would ever pay twenty dollars for a dance done from three feet away. Technically, the cops could have come in at any time and busted us. The word was, however, that there was some type of agreement—bribe, I assumed—that they wouldn't do so in Inkster, MI, where Henry's was located. The owner was an ex-cop, so I assumed he knew what he was doing in that regard.

I asked Stacy about some of my safety and legal concerns, such as how to ensure that a customer was not a cop. She said a lot of it was going with gut feelings, but it was generally understood by customers that they shouldn't ask for specific information about what they were going to get for their time with an escort. Every now and then, she would get a customer who was insistent on knowing what exactly she would do for X amount of money. Although she suspected that those particular guys were not cops, she would cancel the date on the spot just to be safe. The trick was to consistently just use vague language about the kinds of services that were available. I had already noticed that many escorts had disclaimers on their websites, saying something about how all compensation was for their time only and that whatever happened after that was between consenting adults.

I asked Stacy how she had started and she told me she had begun as a stripper and realized she didn't have any issues having sex for money after enough customers kept offering her money for sex. She finally found a guy who wanted to pay her more than she could resist, so she just went with it. She eventually realized she didn't want to work in the club anymore after dealing with too many girls who were doing extras and not charging any additional money for their dances. As far as she was concerned, they were giving it away for way too little.

I asked her about screening customers and how she handled payment. Then I realized I might be annoying and sounding as if I were seeking vicarious thrills by trying to learn more about her life. I had gotten a little of that from friends who asked about my experiences stripping. Stacy said it was no problem at all and she was happy to answer my questions. She said a lot of women entered prostitution without having all the necessary information and it was important to find out about things like safety and how to handle clients. If women didn't take care of each other, who would?

Our conversation continued at the restaurant and was joined by several other escorts. I learned from them the major benefits of working independently instead of with an agency. Escort agencies often took a 50 percent cut, and if a girl knew what she was doing, it was not too hard to make dates and get the whole payment for herself. Some girls would hire a driver for safety, and others used a system with a friend that involved checking in at a specific time after the date with a new customer to ensure their safety. They also sometimes required new clients to give them referrals from other established escorts they had been with so they could call to verify that the guy was safe and was who he said he was. They required clients to make a partial deposit up front to confirm their booking.

I also learned about how these women established their rates. Stacy charged her clients $400 an hour, or $700 for two hours. Brianne, the woman who had given the brilliant stripping presentation, then chimed in to try to convince Stacy to only do two-hour-session minimums. It turned out that Brianne was no longer a stripper but now classified herself as a courtesan, which was basically a very expensive escort. Although she was active in the sex-work community, she did not publicly identify as a prostitute but rather kept up the story that she was an ex-stripper. She had promised her husband not to tell everyone. He did not want the stigma of being married to a woman who had sex for money.

Brianne had a four-hour minimum that started at $2400. She said that it was really all about how you marketed yourself. High-end ladies used terms like "luxury companion" or "private concierge" to describe their services and referred to their encounters as "elite experiences." Many of them also had advanced academic degrees. They emphasized their love of travel and their interest in art and fine cuisine in order to position themselves as a class above the ordinary escort. Brianne said that if an escort gave herself a higher price, clients would assume she was worth that price, and she would subsequently attract men who could afford to pay that amount.

Brianne said that too many women sold themselves for too cheap a price. She considered it her mission to encourage other escorts she met to increase their rates and the minimum amount of time they would spend with someone. It was easier to get more money simply by requiring more time with one client than trying to set up dates with multiple clients for only one hour at a time. Overall, it was a fascinating business plan, but I wasn't sure I had what it took to pull off being an elite escort.

There were a wide variety of women at the table with us. They were all more attractive than average, but that was really the only thing that would have stood out about them as a group, to an outside observer. Everyone was just dressed like a professional woman attending a conference during the summer. They all could've easily been mistaken for the social workers we'd seen earlier that day.

I met another woman named Anna, an ex-escort who was not as happy with her prostitution experience and was now a PhD candidate in anthropology. When she was younger, she had worked for an agency that drove her around all night from job to job. She'd had substance-abuse problems back then but eventually got out and put her life back together. Anna did not personally see prostitution as a positive experience, but she still identified with the women who were in it because of their shared experience. Her position at the conference straddled both worlds. Only the sex workers knew about her past and the other attendees just saw her as an academic who gave a relatively dry anthropological analysis of symbols of prostitution. When I saw her talk the next day, she successfully represented the academic world. No one on the outside would have guessed that she had once been a prostitute.

I ended up learning the stories of most of the women at the table by the end of the night. Finally, a girl who had been relatively quiet throughout dinner started a conversation with me. I had not yet learned what her story was, but she had heard about my experiences with stripping. I asked her what she did, and she said she was a photographer who was interested in doing a project on sex workers, then she asked me if she could photograph me getting ready for work sometime. I understood people's fascination with that type of transformation, but it felt voyeuristic. I realized she had probably just attended the conference to find subjects for her artwork. There probably were women who would be interested in doing a project like that, but I was not one.

I gave her a polite no and she tried to suggest a way that I might feel more comfortable with the idea. So I gave her a firmer no.

At the end of our time at the restaurant, I talked to Stacy about the best way to start getting dates and what a first date would really be like. I could make a website myself, if I wanted to, and base a lot of my copy on the many independent escort sites I had already looked at. I could get pictures taken and blur out my face, which would only emphasize just how discreet I could be. What I wanted to know was how to act the right way on a date. In the strip club, I'd learned to emulate some of the approaches of the women around me, but meeting a client alone did not allow me to see what other women did. I wanted to seem like a confident professional who knew what she was doing. Stacy understood exactly what I was getting at and offered to take me with her on a double sometime. She explained that she liked to travel to Chicago with a girlfriend and had some clients there who liked to be with two women. She said I would be a good match with her because I looked different from her. I was petite with dark hair, and she was tall with blond hair.

As an afterthought, I suddenly realized I should probably talk to the Architect about some of the plans I was making. Stacy gave me her email, and I told her I would get back to her soon. I thanked her for all the information she had given me.

I hadn't actually told the Architect I had begun thinking about escorting. He had been fine with having a stripper girlfriend and had adjusted well to my coming home in the middle of the night. I could tell him customer stories and he didn't blink. He had even visited me in the club and witnessed me talking to tables of other guys and taking them to the back room for private dances. He knew that being with me entailed accepting the fact that I was a sex worker, and he seemed to be doing that well. It didn't seem like too much of a stretch to bring it to the next level, but I would have to see what he thought.

The next day at the conference, I volunteered at one of the registration tables for a few hours. I was responsible for handing out conference materials and telling people where the different presentations were being held. I ended up in a few conversations with different social workers who asked me where I was from and what I did. I kept telling them I was a stripper and was working with Dr. Howard, and I didn't even mention the librarian part because that didn't seem particularly relevant to my identity at the conference.

It was weird to just be open with everyone I talked to for a change. I was far enough removed from my everyday life that I could get away with it. Most of the social workers I talked to just nodded and smiled. They worked with street-level prostitutes who needed help, so they were at the very least trained to refrain from passing moral judgment.

One woman did get into a conversation with me about how I chose to get into stripping and when I explained my decision, she kept asking questions as though she still didn't understand.

I couldn't forget that the goals of a lot of the women in attendance were to get women out of sex work, so there was the weird conflict between sex workers and providers, who typically dealt with women who'd entered prostitution because someone else was making them or because of addiction problems. Many social workers were trained to believe that sex work was always problematic and dehumanizing. It was hard to understand that there were women who entered into it freely and did not see themselves as victims. And, if anything, I think some of the social workers recognized their benefits for prostitutes who made their own decisions, compared to many of the women they helped working on the streets. I had to agree that it was absolutely dehumanizing to have your body used that way if it was not your own choice.

The woman who kept asking me questions began to ask about my customers. How did I feel about giving dances to married men? I pointed out that I did not actively bring married men into the strip club and never tried to push one to buy a dance if he said no.

"But don't you feel bad doing it anyways?" she asked earnestly. "Do you ever think about the guy's wife?"

It was interesting how the tables had turned. A minute before, I was a potential victim of the sex trade. Once she had determined that I had my own agency, I was the predator, and all the poor wives of the married men I preyed on were victims. Did everyone have to be polarized into the victim-predator binary, or could there be a more nuanced explanation for the diverse patterns of human behavior?

I emphasized that men who came into the club chose to do so of their own free will. If they were not getting a dance from me, they would be getting one from someone else. The important distinction, as far as I was concerned was that I did not go out and try to tempt married men to do something they might not already be comfortable with. If I was doing something like that, then I could be blamed for actively creating problems in someone's marriage. I also pointed out that there were couples who came in together to enjoy the entertainment and that not every married man's wife was unaware of his presence in the club. Had she heard of swingers? Not everyone was into heteronormative monogamy. Naturally, she wasn't sure what to make of that.

I met a few more sex worker activists at lunch that day, including one whose moniker I had actually heard of before through my readings on stripping and through other sex workers. She was published and seemed to be one of the leaders in the movement. She had been in the game for a long time and confessed to us that she hadn't had any clients in a year. She was older and bigger, but her identity was so invested in being a sex worker activist that she didn't want to stop engaging in prostitution. I wondered, uncharitably, why she didn't consider retirement. That was unquestionably one of the shitty parts of the game—sex work was really a younger woman's turf. There was room for a few older women, but even then, there were certain limitations. It was too bad more older men didn't prefer women near their own age. She asked the other women to please send clients her way if they came across anyone in her area who they thought might be interested in her.

I finally met someone else who was only a stripper. Then I discovered she was retired and using the fact that she'd once been a stripper to help her with some type of sex worker ministry. I had heard of this phenomenon before. She would go into strip clubs and pass out Jesus-related literature to help "save" the women working there. Her ministry also included some type of financial support system to help women get out of the business. She considered her experiences stripping to have been bad, the result of drug use and of not having Jesus in her life. From my perspective, it was weird when someone thought they had no way to control their life until they began believing in some specific religious dogma. People like that equated faith with being able to really make their own decisions, and I saw it as doing the opposite.

As much as I didn't like her mission, she did not act as though her conversion made her better than anyone else. Presumably, that was why she was able to be so open about being a former stripper. When all the sex workers were gathering at the end of the conference to take a picture, she wanted to jump in too—and I surprised myself by doing so as well. Despite all my fears about my double life, there is a picture somewhere out there of me with a bunch of cool prostitutes and a Jesus-loving stripper.

Later that night, when I got back home and saw the Architect, I told him about all the amazing women I had met and how I wanted to try to break into high-end escorting. I didn't expect his reaction—he was really surprised and considered the whole idea to be a big problem. My initial reaction was that maybe he just needed some time to get used to it. I talked to him about it again a few days later and he was still not at all into the idea. He told me he knew stripping was a given. He had met me doing it and would never ask me to stop. But he had not signed up for prostitution. He worried about the legal ramifications, but more than that, he just didn't want me having sex with anyone else. Somehow, I hadn't thought that he would react so strongly.

I had to decide what I wanted to do. Part of me felt that I should have the freedom to do whatever I wanted and that having a man put restrictions on my choices was oppressive. But the more I thought about it, the more I understood where he was coming from. He had handled being a stripper's boyfriend better than I thought anyone ever would, but then again, I wasn't really giving men a high bar.

Part of the reason escorting had appealed to me was that my earnings at Henry's were getting increasingly inconsistent. My underlying motivating factor in all of these sex work ventures had always been to remove my debt. I just wanted to take the fastest possible route to eradicating it and I was sure I could do it much faster on my back. I would have to find a way to accept that it would just be a longer process. I also considered that if things did not work out with the Architect, I had some new opportunities open to me. But as long as I was with him, I agreed not to do it—which ended up being forever. Looking back now, I regret not standing my ground and joining the awesome escort cabal I had met.

Eventually, Dr. Howard and I collaborated with some professors at a few different universities and found our specific stripping-related research project. A few years later, we got an article published in a major academic journal. That was good for my career, in theory, and I might have considered putting the article on my résumé if I'd been interested in working in an academic library. I could have pointed to it as an example of my involvement in scholarly research, but then I would have had to find a way to field any questions about exactly how I got into that kind of research, especially considering that Dr. Howard taught at a different university than the one I'd attended for my library degree.

As I was only interested in public libraries, I could not see any practical applications to listing myself as a coauthor of the article on my résumé. I only told a few friends and always had to wonder what people I knew professionally would have thought if they'd found it in a database with my name attached.

20

------◄◆○◆►------

Later that summer, there was an influx of new girls, and they just got younger and younger. I was only twenty-five but was beginning to feel edged out by a bunch of nineteen-year-olds. Part of the problem was that customers often wanted to try the new girl. I was beginning to feel like old hat. I knew that was the cyclical nature of things, and some of my customers would probably eventually come back—but it was messing with my confidence.

I worried that I might be turning too much into a buddy with my customers and might be having trouble maintaining a long-term fantasy with some men. One guy, in particular, stood out in this regard. He was an engineer with thick glasses, and we had bonded over the fact that we had both stayed in Michigan for relationships when we knew we had better employment prospects in other states. While my relationship was still going strong, his had ended up not working out. He was one of the customers I genuinely enjoyed talking to, and I could tell he felt the same way about me. But then one day, he only wanted to talk to me while paying for dances from one of the new young girls. I wondered if I had just gotten too real with him, disrupting his ability to see me as an object of his fantasy.

I felt as though my hustle was beginning to break, and I realized I was going home and crying at least once a week because I hadn't made enough money that night. I had been doing so well just a few months before, and I couldn't quite put my finger on what had changed.

The problem could have been the five pounds I had gained by going a little crazy at the buffets in Vegas. I knew intellectually that five pounds shouldn't have made that much of a difference—Autumn and Cherry were both bigger girls, and they still made out well most nights—but it might have been affecting my confidence in how I looked.

I also wondered if being in a relationship was affecting my hustle. I had thought balancing my dual identities as a stripper and a librarian was complicated, but in a way, it was more difficult navigating being in an intimate relationship and then going to work and feigning intimacy with a bunch of strangers. Maybe it had been easier to be someone's temporary pretend girlfriend when I wasn't someone's real girlfriend.

I also considered that part of my problem might have been the identity shift I had undergone from being Penelope—grad student, moonlighting as a stripper—to Penelope, failed librarian who had to be a stripper because she was a failure. Although I was still working at Suburban, my ten hours a week weren't enough to make me feel as though I really belonged to the profession.

On nights when I was striking out left and right, I had one fun thing left. On those nights, it wasn't usually a problem finding men who wanted to hang out with me, but rather, it was hard to find men who wanted to buy dances and make my time with them worthwhile. Whenever I encountered someone who had made it clear that he had no intention of buying a dance from me but still wanted me to sit at his table and "get to know him," I would just take advantage of the opportunity and begin ruining the fantasy for him. One time, a table of younger guys told me they weren't buying dances but wanted to know what I was doing after work. I happily told them exactly what I was really planning on doing. "I'm putting on comfy pants and watching an episode of *Star Trek: The Next Generation*." They began trying to convince me that this was a lame thing to do, and I just kept talking about *Star Trek*. Then one guy even tried to play this game back with me by feigning interest in *Star Trek* but ended up making *Star Wars* references instead.

I hit rock bottom one night when another girl in the dressing room brought in a twenty-ounce coke bottle filled with nothing but Jägermeister. She told me I could drink as much of it as I liked. I had already finished my usual half-pint, but after working the floor and not really getting anywhere, I wandered back into the dressing room and took a few chugs of her Jäger. I repeated that pattern several more times, and by the end of the night, I was ridiculously inebriated.

I was too drunk, and I even went and told the manager that I felt ill so I wouldn't have to go onstage for the rest of the night. I called the Architect a few times and told him I was really drunk, and he offered to come pick me up. I told him I would be fine and would ask Amber, who also lived in Ypsilanti, to give me a ride home. Amber told me she would take me home and was glad I had asked instead of trying to drive home myself.

I went back to the dressing room to wait for Amber to take me home. It was one thirty, so there was only a half hour to go. I changed out of my stripper outfit and put my street clothes on. By 1:40, I had become unreasonably impatient and began freaking out. I really wanted to be out of Henry's, and I kept fixating on how I didn't want to leave my car in the parking lot overnight. Suddenly, I found myself stumbling out of the parking lot and getting into my car—somehow justifying that ridiculous action to myself. As I drove off, I called the Architect and told him that I was coming to him and that I had taken my car so I would have it the next day.

He told me I needed to pull over immediately and wait for him to come get me. I complained that there was nowhere nearby to pull over that wasn't dark and abandoned. Then I promised him I would stop at the next gas station I saw that was open. I knew there were several on Michigan Avenue. He told me to get off the phone so I could concentrate on driving as safely as possible until I could pull over.

When I pulled into the first gas station I encountered, I thought I was just fine. My freak-out had passed, and for some asinine reason, I thought the whole situation was funny. I got out of my car, called the Architect, and told him where I was. When he asked what the nearest cross street was, I told him "Princess Elizabeth." I have no fucking clue what was going through my mind when I said that.

I heard him confer with someone and asked who was with him. He told me he had to go and would be there as soon as he could. I sat on the curb and continued to feel high levels of amusement with myself. Eventually I got a call from Amber—she had gotten my number from another girl, and she wanted to make sure I was okay. I told her I'd left but the Architect had made me pull over and I was waiting for him.

I had to wait forever, and when he finally showed up, he was pretty mad. He explained that he had jumped straight in his car and raced to get to me but had been pulled over by a police officer for speeding. He told me there was no Princess Elizabeth Street and that the police officer didn't even know what he was talking about. Luckily, he had allowed the Architect to go with only a warning.

"Where did you get Princess Elizabeth from?"

I was doubled over laughing and having trouble breathing because I thought it was so funny. Finally, I said I knew there was an Elizabeth Street somewhere farther down Michigan Avenue, which I later looked up and found was true.

"Where did you get the 'Princess' from, then?" he asked, understandably confused.

"I don't know."

The Architect moved my car to a nearby hotel's parking lot, and I got into his passenger seat for him to drive me back to his house.

The next day, I woke up feeling like the biggest, most pathetic asshole. There was no way I should have been driving that night, and there was no excuse for my behavior. I had gotten way too drunk at work, and while I had multiple safe ways to get home, I had bypassed all of them to get behind the wheel anyway. I would have to keep my drinking in better check in the future. I was very lucky that I hadn't gotten into an accident that hurt someone, or worse, killed someone.

I deserved to have gotten pulled over that night instead of the Architect. I had already been pulled over twice for speeding while driving home from Henry's and had managed to get off with warnings both times after I successfully recited the alphabet backward at an acceptable speed. I would have failed that task miserably had I been pulled over that night.

The Princess Elizabeth incident—as we came to call it—was symptomatic of my bigger issues. I needed a change of pace. I had to vary things up somehow and get my hustle back. First, I tried working a day shift and then stayed for a double, just to do something different. I convinced myself that if I were there for fourteen hours straight, I would have to make good money. I only ended up making $250, which would have been okay for a single shift but was pretty bad for a double. I lost steam by ten at night, and after that point, I couldn't hustle to save my life.

I finally considered that what I really needed to do was to just try another club altogether. I needed to get out and experience a few different clubs and expand my options. There were something like thirty clubs in Detroit proper, but I was still against the idea of getting a dance card and having my name put into a database. I had heard some good things about the new Pantheon Club in Dearborn, so I decided to give it a try one night. Pantheon was fancier than Henry's—which was really not hard to achieve—with all sorts of Ionic columns and velvet draperies as part of its decor. The club was bigger than Henry's and had a much more inviting atmosphere, with a good main stage. I even bumped into another girl I knew who had worked at Henry's for a while. It occurred to me that it would probably be impossible for me at that point to walk into a club in metro Detroit and not know at least someone there, be that another girl or a customer.

My night went by without incident. The DJ announced me onstage, saying it was my first time stripping ever—he warned me he would do this ahead of time—and that was pretty beneficial for my stage tips. I found a good customer near the beginning of the night and, because of my insecurity in a new club, probably spent too much time with him. Another customer got several dances from me as well. If I had put more effort into hustling, though, I probably could have done better. I had a decent night but nothing to get too excited about. I left, intending to go back sometime soon.

I also decided to try Deja Vu, the strip club chain that had a club in Ypsilanti, where I was living. I had previously dismissed Deja Vu as too close to home to consider working at when I was living in Ann Arbor. Now, I lived even closer to where I was working, but I was no longer that worried about anyone seeing me. I was out of school, and I just didn't care anymore.

The other consideration with working at Deja Vu was that it was a full-nude club. When I first thought about becoming a stripper, that was a big deal. I'd even had friends who approved of my choice to become a stripper because I was "only doing topless." But at that point, the few square inches of fabric that I wore after taking off my clothes onstage every night did not seem like a big deal.

I had also ruled them out before because they did not do house fees but required strippers to give one-third of everything they made to the house. I still wasn't very comfortable with that idea, realizing that on the best night I'd ever had at Henry's, making $600, I only had to give up $100 in fees—and only $80 on a normal night. If I had this kind of night at the Vu, I would have to give up $200. But I hadn't made anywhere near that in a while.

There was also a completely different approach to hustling at the Vu. The Architect and I had visited before as customers and had observed how the girls were actively encouraged after each finale to walk around the club and ask as many people as they could, during a three-minute song, if they would like to get a dance. This was called the "wanna dance?" approach, which I had always assumed most customers didn't like. Yet when we were there, I observed lots of guys go back with the girls who used the "wanna dance?" approach. I was also interested in the Vu because they had stricter rules about contact. Customers could touch the girls, but there were a lot of limitations, and the rules were actively enforced.

The auditions at Deja Vu were more elaborate than at any other club in the area. They took place only on amateur night, which was once a week. Many people were surprised to learn that the women who participated in amateur night contests were usually just strippers who worked at other clubs. Sometimes there were actual amateurs in those contests, but they usually got beaten out by the experienced strippers. The incentive for women to compete was usually a cash prize, and at Deja Vu, it was $300.

On the night of my amateur-night audition, only two other girls showed up to compete. One was a stripper from Jackson, and the other was her friend who worked in the same club as a waitress. Objectively, I knew they were both better looking than me. My only goal was not to get last place in the contest, so that was what made me the most nervous. Deja Vu didn't actually care which place you came in as far as their hiring decisions were concerned, though. They just required that anyone compete, if they wanted to work there. It was probably their way of ensuring that enough people participated in the contest, which they advertised weekly.

The Jackson stripper went first, I went second, and her waitress friend went last. Our rankings were determined by how loud the audience cheered for each of us. The Jackson stripper got first place, which was what I expected. I got second place, beating out the waitress, which wouldn't have happened had she known what she was doing—she had spent most of her set glued to the pole, averting her eyes from the audience.

Then we were invited back to the manager's office to collect our winnings—second place was twenty-five whole dollars—and offered jobs to work at the Vu. I said I was interested, so the manager asked when I would be ready to be put on the schedule. I told him the next week would be fine, and he gave me some forms to fill out.

I learned that I had to work a minimum of four shifts a week, and one of them had to be day shift. There was also a rule about not working at any other clubs, although the manager explained this rule in such a way as to suggest he didn't really care as long as it didn't interfere with my regular shifts and I didn't advertise it.

I wasn't sure I wanted to commit to four shifts a week right off the bat—I had enjoyed the freedom of coming and going as I pleased at Henry's—but then again, I needed a change, so I decided to go along with it. I could always quit and move along if I didn't like it there.

On my first night, I did reasonably well. In part, that was due to the success of getting a young customer with some disposable cash who was relatively new to visiting strip clubs. He was just happy to keep buying dance after dance without expecting more or spewing any annoying bullshit. I had psyched myself up and successfully worked the entire night without a single drink as well, which I considered a major accomplishment.

Despite being a full-nude club, there was something much more wholesome about Deja Vu than the others clubs I had worked at and visited in the metro Detroit area. That might have been in part because it was designated as a "juice bar" and did not serve any alcohol. It was common for cities that allowed strip clubs to have rules about mixing full nudity with alcohol—as though combining the two would create too much debauchery or something. As a result, clubs that served alcohol were typically topless and full-nude venues were mostly alcohol-free.

Since we were actual employees, we were given one formal break a night when we were allowed to leave the building—but only if we demonstrated to the manager that we had a buddy. We took advantage of that and a girl who wanted a break that entailed leaving the building would pair up with another girl based on her "interests." Some girls would leave to smoke pot in one of their cars. Others, including me, would go to the bar a few doors down and pound shots. My two main drinking break buddies were an Eastern Michigan sociology major and a University of Michigan English major who said she started stripping because her ADHD was too bad for her to be good at waitressing. We only had about fifteen minutes, so there wasn't enough time for me to get more than a little buzzed, which was probably for the best.

Something about the general environment of the Vu was less sad and hopeless than Henry's. For one thing, the managers actually talked to us and seemed to be friendly. They were not sitting at the bar—the juice bar—staring into space sullenly all night. One manager who looked and acted like a teddy bear exemplified that difference when he came into work one day and told me enthusiastically how he knew it was going to be a good day because he had danced with his cat to the radio that morning.

Most of the girls I met at the Vu were less jaded than the girls I had met at other clubs. For many of them, this was the first club they had ever worked at. Most were pretty young, and I only met a few who had the obligation of children. The oldest girl I met was thirty and often referred to herself as a "thirty-year-old stripper" as though that were an odd thing, which it certainly had not been at Henry's.

There were also a lot more girls who were in college. At Henry's, the only girl who was in school was Amber, who was studying nursing at Eastern Michigan. There was more of a feeling of hope for a better future amongst many of the girls at the Vu. That was sort of refreshing, and I had not fully realized how the mood of Henry's had been affecting me.

I even met another girl I could fully qualify as more awkward than me. I only worked with her when I was required to work the day shifts, because that was when she preferred to work. Somehow in conversation it came up that she had twelve cats. I made the mistake of asking her how she had gotten so many, and she reported back in detail the provenance of all twelve of them. It was a slow day, and I couldn't come up with a good excuse to get away.

The Vu girls were also significantly more acrobatic onstage and skilled on the pole. I had never actually had the opportunity to practice using the pole without an audience in front of me, but it was often possible during a slow day shift, when there were no customers, to have both time and instruction to try new things on the pole. I had only done basic spins before, but I learned to climb the pole and then slide down it upside down.

There was one girl who had been Miss Nude Ohio a year or two before, which the DJ always announced when she came onstage. The poles at the Vu went up to the ceiling, at least twenty feet. She would climb all the way to the top of one and hang on it sideways with only one leg. Her performances were always interesting because she was so athletic, but at the same time, she did everything with a clinical gaze on her face. Although she was completely naked, there was nothing sexy to me about the way she danced.

Overall, everyone was much more theatrical and enthusiastic onstage at the Vu. My favorite performances were by a girl who routinely liked to dance to Lords of Acid's "Sit on My Face," and she would writhe erotically on the ground during the orgasm portions of the song.

I had gotten lazy in the music department. The Vu DJ kept asking me what I wanted to have played when I was on stage, and I told him I didn't care. I had gotten used to having to dance to Nickleback, and once I'd done that, I could dance to anything. On my first night, I said Depeche Mode, so while I was at the Vu, the DJ played a lot of Depeche Mode when it was my turn onstage. I had been an obnoxious music snob in college, but a lot of what I liked did not necessarily translate well to stripping, so I didn't bother trying to pick something distinctive.

I had also gotten lazy in enforcing some of the safety precautions I had instituted at the beginning of my stripping career. I realized that one day while I was talking to the manager of the porn shop attached to the Vu. He had started a conversation with me by saying that we lived in the same apartment complex, which he had observed the other night when he had driven home behind me. I wasn't worried at all about this guy, but talking to him made me realize I hadn't been watching the cars in my rearview mirror to make sure I wasn't being followed like I used to. It was more important than ever that I remember to stay aware, considering how much closer I lived to the club now. It was a lot easier for a potential creeper to follow me home, as I only lived about five miles away.

A lot of younger customers came into the Vu. That was due to the fact that you only had to be eighteen to enter and also because it was so close to Eastern Michigan University's campus. The Vu was open until four in the morning, and a lot of people would come in at two o'clock when the bars closed. Drunk college kids were not really my forte, so I tended to approach guys who looked more like adults.

I did give a dance to the most adorable eighteen-year-old-looking couple once, though. The girl had come up to me holding a lollipop and had asked me shyly if they could buy a dance from me. They sat side-by-side and had the most amazed innocent expressions on their faces as the girl continued to suck on her lollipop. For once, I didn't mind that someone only bought one dance, because afterward they smiled enthusiastically and repeatedly thanked me.

My most devoted, submissive customer—Peter, from Henry's— came into see me one night. He had apparently been going into Henry's and just sitting around until Cherry told him I was working at the Vu now. He bought a VIP room from me, which was one of the Vu's private rooms that were pretty hard to sell. I spent most of the time giving him various instructions and having him worship my feet. I found out that there was a camera in the room when one of the managers later told me how much she had laughed watching us.

Since I was working closer to Ann Arbor, it was inevitable that I would be encountering more people from the University of Michigan. One night, I gave some dances to a Michigan economics professor, and I asked him if he knew one of my professors at the School of Information, because I knew some of them had economics backgrounds. I could tell he was surprised and uncomfortable with the close association—he had probably thought it was safe to assume a stripper wouldn't know his colleagues. I reassured him that I had been a student at the School of Information and none of my professors had known I was a stripper.

Then another night, a student who had been in my program came in. I had just come back from my break, and when I returned to the floor, I saw him seated with friends at the stage. He had concentrated in human-computer interaction, which seems like an important distinction for me to point out, because I could never imagine any of the male librarians I had met going to a strip club. I had worked with him on a semester-long group project and, as with some of the other students I had worked with at SI, I had to edit the hell out of his contributions to our papers.

My initial reaction was the beginning of an adrenaline-fueled anxiety attack. I stumbled into the dressing room and took a deep breath, but at that point, I'd learned it was better to confront my fear head-on. It was one thing to have someone in my program know I stripped, but it was another for one of them to actually see me. There was nowhere I could stand out on the floor where he would not turn around and observe me and know instantaneously who I was. I decided to take the initiative in controlling my own fear. I would rather be found out on my own terms than worry about possibly being recognized, so I walked straight to him and sat down next to him and said "Hi."

He turned to me and said "Hi" back and then asked me how I was doing that night.

"You don't recognize me?" I was sure he couldn't have had that understated of a response if he really knew who I was.

He looked at me critically and shook his head, embarrassed. "I'm sorry. Can you help me out? Give me a clue."

I was genuinely surprised. It was really hard to gauge how different I looked in real life from how I looked dressed up as Penelope. Apparently, there was a bigger difference than I'd thought. I might have gotten up and walked away without him ever placing me, but then again, he could have put two and two together later. If anything, he'd have the incentive to try to figure out who I was now that I had come up to him and insinuated that we knew each other.

I told him my name and then the name of the class we had worked an entire semester together on.

"Oh, hey," he said, finally seeing who I was. "Yeah, I totally didn't recognize you." He was surprised but not as surprised as I thought he would be.

I ended up offering him a dance, which was probably a mistake, because I think we both felt a little weird after I gave it, or at least I know I did. It had become such a habit to offer dances to all the guys

I talked to that I hadn't stopped to think about how this might have been one of those times when it would actually have been better not to. He didn't come in again, so it didn't end up being a problem, and a year or two later, he actually contacted me for some help editing his dissertation.

My big switch to working at the Vu didn't help my money for long. I had good nights, but overall, it was getting harder and harder for me to hustle. I spent most of one night helping edit some work the Architect was working on in the locker room in order to avoid working the floor. I found that the "wanna dance" finales were just too depressing. It was hard to wander around the room and ask as many guys as possible if they wanted a dance in such a short time period. I would usually try about three guys and then give up.

I was beginning to feel an even greater sense of futility listening to some of the girls talking in the dressing room. Like the girls at Henry's who had been in the business for years, there were a few high-earning veterans at the Vu. When I heard them complaining on bad nights about how good it used to be and how they were having bad nights, I would feel that it was even more hopeless for me to try. I would just get to a point where I had heard enough *no*s for one night and needed a break from it all.

My breaking point came one time when I realized that some drunken college boys had thrown quarters onto the stage where I was dancing. I turned and saw that they were laughing and very pleased with themselves, but all I could do was give them a dirty look. It was easy to overanalyze what that meant. I was only worth a quarter compared to the usual dollar people tipped with on the stage? Or were they just drunk and that was the only money they had so they threw it at me because it was better than nothing? Regardless, I did not bend over to pick up my quarters and left the stage, furious, when my set was up.

Weekend nights were the busiest but the worst for me because the customers were mostly cheap college kids. In college I had stayed away from frat culture, so I didn't know how to navigate it as an adult, nor did I want to. I also was having trouble working the incredibly slow day shifts when a customer wouldn't come in for an hour at a time. I had been at the Vu for less than two months, but the itch to move on was coming to me again.

21

---◆○◆---

I never formally quit the Vu—I just decided to wander back into Henry's one night. I actually received a pretty warm reception from my coworkers, and even Fred expressed excitement at seeing me, which was a major compliment because he was the least enthusiastic person I knew.

The money continued to remain unsteady. One of the owner's sons was managing some shifts now, and I quickly decided I didn't like him. He was young and less jaded than the rest of Henry's management, but his enthusiasm came off as obnoxious. One discount dance night, I was sitting at the bar, waiting till my next stage set, and he told me I should go hustle.

"I already know all these guys," I told him. "They either don't buy dances or are waiting for someone else."

"Well, you won't sell dances with that attitude! You never know. You should go talk to them."

"Seriously, I know they won't buy dances. I'm waiting for some other customers to come in the door."

"Seriously, don't sit at the bar. Look busy!" He gave me a fake smile.

I slinked off to go sit in the dressing room instead.

As a last resort to get my hustle going again, I considered trying some out-of-state clubs. The stripper message boards were full of great trip reports by girls who had traveled and danced in various cities. The best easy money seemed to be at clubs in less populated areas such as Montana and Oklahoma. I wasn't ready to travel that far, but I was willing to try Chicago, so I planned a visit to my parents. I told them I would be getting in late due to work, and then I worked one night at Club 390 in Chicago Heights. It was an okay night, and I planned to try to work at least three other nights there while I was in town, but I made the mistake of telling my sister what I had been doing.

I had already told her that I was working as a stripper, so I didn't expect that telling her I was working temporarily in Chicagoland would be that big of a deal. Instead, she got really mad and proceeded to give me a lecture about what a loser I was and say that I should find a better way to support myself because lots of other people managed to take on student loan debt and not become strippers. By the end of the conversation, I was crying, and I had to call the Architect to help calm me down.

After that, I didn't feel up to working the other days I had planned during my visit. I was mad at myself for not being able to just get over it and go to work anyway. Instead, I spent the rest of the trip lounging around my parents' house and did not do much of anything.

By the time I got back to Michigan, I knew I was going to have to figure something out. I was beginning to feel as though I really needed a break from stripping, but I had not been making enough money lately to justify not working for a while, especially since I had also not managed to find a roommate yet. I was still paying for a two-bedroom apartment every month. I had met with one girl who was interested in the apartment, but I might have scared her off when I said I was a strip club waitress—at least that was near the truth, but, I thought, potentially not as problematic. I had met another girl on the stripper message boards who was interested in moving to the area from Lansing and often worked at the Playhouse in Romulus. She would have been my ideal roommate, but then she decided she needed to live closer to the northern suburbs of Detroit.

I had also started looking at library jobs in Michigan but had not seen any posted for a full-time position in months, so I did not have a lot of faith that my library career was going to take off anytime soon. It looked as though my best prospect would be to try to get a waitressing job again, which might tide me over until I could build up the energy to become an enthusiastic stripper again. I also considered that I should keep the waitressing job and just strip occasionally to supplement my income.

During all of that time, the Architect was well aware of my worries. He offered to have me move in with him and just cancel the lease on my apartment. I wanted to do that, but I was also worried that if I quit stripping, I would not make enough money to pay for my share of the living expenses. I really hated the idea of becoming financially dependent on him, not because I didn't trust him but because it would make me feel like more of a failure if I could not even manage to take care of myself.

Finally, I told him I was thinking about quitting stripping, and he gave me the best possible response. He told me that he thought that was a good idea because he was tired of seeing me so stressed out all the time. He also said he'd been hoping I would decide that at some point. I was impressed because he had managed to keep those feelings to himself. He hadn't wanted to pressure me to stop stripping because he had met me that way, and he didn't feel it was his place to tell me what he thought I should do. I told him I was worried about making enough money, and he said he didn't care. He just wanted to be with me, and all that mushy romantic stuff.

Essentially, the Architect would be my safety net if I needed him to be. I was a little worried that this would put me into sugar-daddy territory, which was something I had strived hard to avoid. But at the same time, I had to make some changes, for my own sanity.

I began applying for waitressing jobs everywhere. I got one interview at a Romano's Macaroni Grill, but I could tell that I did not successfully convince the manager that I would be able to stay for a long time. I stopped mentioning my master's degree on the applications and finally got a job at a nice restaurant in Ann Arbor. Unfortunately, they wanted me to work the breakfast and lunch shifts, when the food was much less expensive. But I was willing to take the job with the hope that I could eventually move up to the dinner shift and make decent tip money.

I worked my last night stripping without knowing it would really be my last night. It was the Wednesday before Thanksgiving, and I made almost $400. In retrospect, it was a good night to go out on. I had intended to stop back in and work again at some point, but it never actually happened.

At all the waitressing jobs I'd had before, I had worked either lunch or night shifts. I wasn't a morning person, so it was an adjustment to get up at five-thirty in the morning four days a week to help open a restaurant for breakfast. The restaurant was attached to a hotel, and how busy it was varied. Some days, I spent most of my time standing around, talking to the other bored servers, watching Good Morning America on the TV mounted above the bar, while doing Sudoku. I didn't make very much money, but I knew that the servers who worked the night shift did pretty well, so I figured I just needed to bide my time.

Getting up so early, though, made the whole idea of working a shift stripping until two in the morning really unappealing, even if I had the next day off at the restaurant. Plus, I still had my shifts at Suburban to account for. The other factor that had kept me from going back was that I had managed to quit smoking again, and I was afraid to be in a bar setting, where I would be tempted to start again. Quitting smoking had also brought on the weight gain I seemed to get whenever I quit, which was another deterrent to my thinking about getting naked for money again.

I only went back into Henry's again a few months later to drop off a Prada wallet that a sweet younger stripper named Holly had insisted I watch for her. She had maxed out three credit cards and wanted me to hang on to it for her so she wouldn't spend any more money. I thought it was a bad idea, but she said I was the only one she could trust to keep it safe and she would tell me when she was ready to take it back. Going back into Henry's was a little weird. There were already a bunch of new girls I didn't recognize and I didn't stay long.

I also got a wild call from Heaven telling me she had found the coat that had been stolen from my locker. The one time I had accidentally left my locker unlocked for just an hour, my coat had disappeared. A group of random girls had come in to work that night, so I figured one of them had probably taken it and I would never see them or my coat again. Heaven had started working at another club, and she swore one of those girls was working there. She had taken my coat back from the girl and wanted me to come pick it up sometime. I highly suspected that the coat she had stolen wasn't mine and she had just stolen some poor girl's coat for no reason. When the coat was stolen, it was only the second time I'd worn it to Henry's, so I really doubted Heaven knew what my coat looked like. I did not go get the coat.

I stayed in contact with Nick for a while. He had helped me move into my last apartment, so I promised to pay him back by helping him with a website he wanted to make. The last time I talked to him, some years later, I asked him about all the girls I used to work with, and none of them were working there anymore.

When I switched to waitressing, I placed a greater focus on upgrading my résumé. I was working on my web-development skills and, at Suburban, was offering to help with as many projects as I could. It was always so awkward during interviews when people asked if I had done something and I had to tell them no and then try to say something trite about being confident that I could do whatever it was, which never sounded very convincing, especially coming from me. At Suburban, I was able to start weeding the collection, which gave me collection-development experience, and begin planning children's story times.

I began applying for the part-time librarian positions because they seemed to be the only postings that I ever saw come up in Southeastern Michigan. I had made the mistake of thinking they were beneath my $80,000 master's degree at first, but I was no longer in a position to be picky and was beginning to realize this was just the part-timing of the profession. In order to save money, many libraries were splitting positions in half so they were not legally required to pay benefits.

I went through a series of interviews that did not seem to get anywhere. At the very least, I knew there was nothing wrong with my résumé and cover letter, because I got calls for most of the jobs I applied for. I was beginning to think, though, that I gave a bad first impression. I was probably too nervous going into these interviews and, as a result, was coming off without enough confidence to impress anyone.

At one library, the director asked me—while eating a pudding cup—how I could demonstrate that I would be happy staying in a part-time position and not eventually leave for something full-time. I thought I had given pretty good answers to everything else she had asked, but I couldn't find the right way to answer that question. I told her I already had my job at Suburban, so between the two of them, that should be enough for me. Then she probed further about whether I would really be tempted by a full-time opportunity if it came up. I ended up just telling her I didn't know, because that wasn't a situation that I'd been in. I wondered if the right answer was to say I was being supported by a man, while I pursued my hobby career and that I just didn't want to work that much anyway. Or should I have said I had young children and didn't want to work full-time? She had asked me, after all, if I had or wanted kids, which I was pretty sure was an illegal question. But then again, maybe you didn't have follow legal protocols at an informal pudding interview.

One interview in which I put my foot in my mouth repeatedly was conducted by a panel of three librarians, two in upper administration and one who was in charge of the library's website. The position had been specifically advertised as a part-time adult services position, with responsibilities that involved also helping with the website. In the beginning, while they were looking over my résumé, one of them frowned and said, "Oh, you went to Michigan? We all went to Wayne State," while pointing at the rest of the women on the panel. They all reminisced about how much they had enjoyed going to Wayne State and then they looked at me as if they felt sorry for me. I had no idea what the point behind that was. If the fact that I went to Michigan was a problem, then they shouldn't have called me for an interview, I thought. I hadn't hidden the fact that I went there or left it off my résumé. All I could do was shrug and try to smile awkwardly.

I further scored the webmaster librarian's disapproval when I said I had never used Second Life—a virtual, online world where people could interact with each other as avatars. She was sure that Second Life was going to be the hot new thing in libraries and consequently thought it was important for everyone in the profession to be experienced with it. Obviously, that never happened and for good reason.

But our real clashes came when we began discussing the mechanics of web development. She said she was looking for someone who could turn their homepage's navigation into drop-down menus with JavaScript. I offered that it would be better to do it with CSS because that would make it more accessible. She did not like that answer, which I thought was weird, because from looking at the code on that library's site, she clearly knew neither technology. What is the point of having a preference when you don't even know how it works? I thought. Finally, the director asked me what I would do to improve their website, and I offered that I would like to make some changes to improve usability, such as having the same navigation on every page of the site—you know, pretty standard stuff. The webmaster librarian quickly interjected, "But it is usable!" I had insulted her poorly designed website and basically hammered in the last nail in my own coffin with that job.

I left that interview feeling more frustrated than I had ever felt after an interview. I completely overreacted and stopped at a gas station on my way back home to buy a pack of cigarettes ruining my four months of not smoking. I later learned that they had hired one of their interns, so the job was probably that person's to begin with. It had seemed completely ridiculous to me that she wanted to find someone to help her fix their website but then pretend that wasn't because she lacked the skill set to do it herself. I took solace in knowing there was no way I could have done that job correctly anyway without also stomping on that lady's ego.

I did have an interview for one of the very few full-time jobs I saw advertised. That position also involved working on the website. I felt pretty good after the interview, but I knew better than to get too excited. Time passed, and I knew I was not likely to receive a call from them, but I did get a very encouraging rejection letter. It was a typical rejection form letter, but the director had handwritten a note on it, telling me that it had been a very close choice between me and one other person. She also wanted to encourage me to apply for anything else they posted in the future. Of course, I agonized a little about what I'd said that gave the other person ultimately more of an edge over me, but in general, I felt more confident that I wasn't doing everything completely wrong after all.

I had several other interviews and some second interviews. More than a year after I graduated, I was still working at Suburban and the hotel restaurant. I still hadn't moved up to the night shift, and then I found out that one of the servers who had been hired after me—and also had less serving experience—was moving up before me. I asked the management about this, and they said that I needed to have more consistent availability in order to move up. The hours I worked at Suburban varied a lot, and I always had to give the restaurant different blocks of availability every week as a result.

I was trying to contribute to the household expenses with the Architect but it was kind of a joke. I only paid for the cable and Internet bill and bought the groceries. I never actually handed him any money directly, and I felt bad about it. I could never afford to pay when we went out to eat, except for one time when I took us out for a fancy dinner at the Big Boy. None of that seemed to bother the Architect, though, and he said I should just quit my no-money restaurant job so I didn't have to get up so early and then be so tired after my shifts. Basically, he thought my contribution was such a pittance that it barely even helped, and he'd rather have me happier. That was a tempting offer, but then I would officially be some chick completely mooching off a man.

During this time, I had also been taking web design and development classes at the local community college. Not only was I hoping it would improve my résumé, but the very fact that I was enrolled in an institution of higher learning allowed me to keep deferring my student loans—I didn't have to pay them until I was no longer in school. Initially, I took advantage of that, but at the end of the day, my student loan debt stressed me out too much just let it sit there, so I had begun making the minimum payments that would be required if they hadn't been deferred.

Finally, I made the difficult decision that the best thing to do financially would be to quit Suburban. I had already gotten two years of experience there and wasn't likely to actually do anything new if I stayed. Despite my job title change, I was still only making the library aide's $10.38 an hour, instead of the librarian wage. It wasn't enough money to justify giving up the opportunity to work the night shift at the restaurant, especially when I had been making barely above minimum wage on the day shift. Talking to night shift servers, I knew I would probably at least triple my income working at night.

So I informed the director of Suburban, and she said she was sad to see me go. I explained that I just couldn't get the shifts I needed to make enough money with the variable schedule, and she said she understood. Soon after I had finished my training to work the night shift, though, the director called me back to offer me a twenty-hour-a-week job with a consistent schedule as well as a bump up to the librarian wage. I gladly accepted and, after talking to the Architect, decided to also quit the restaurant job. I would be making the same amount I made working minimum wage, but I'd be working half the amount of time. I decided I would use the extra time to further pursue web development coursework at the community college when the new semester started in the fall. Web design was beginning to look like a viable backup plan to not getting a full-time job as a librarian, and I wanted to expand my options.

Then, two months later, I did get a bona fide full-time librarian job. It had been almost a year and a half since I'd graduated, but it finally happened. It was another librarian position that also focused on the library's website. The library was in the area, and everyone informed me it was notorious for its high turnover, but I didn't care because it was a full-time job and I would finally have benefits. I would later learn that a lot of this library's reputation was due to the revolving door of directors and board members.

I was interviewed by the director, the head of adult services, and the IT person. The director seemed to be playing good cop while the head of adult services seemed to be playing bad cop, and the IT person kept trying to trick me. It made me more nervous than usual, but at the end of the day, I got the job because I was the only one they interviewed who successfully demonstrated the ability to code on command.

Later, I would say I had taken "the brute force approach," especially to other library school grads looking for advice about how to find a job. By developing skills that were not as common among many applicants, I positioned myself in such a way that eventually some library somewhere would want me even if I didn't always say the right thing during the pressures of a first interview.

My whole experience with the job search made me paranoid about my employability. I had never considered that it would be that hard. The promotional material that the School of Information had sent me before I started, had touted all the amazing jobs their grads got straight out of school. At my new library, I made sure to get involved in as many programs and departments as possible so I could gain further experience, as well as be seen as an irreplaceable member of the staff. I kind of went on a wild skill-grabbing binge. I wasn't satisfied not being in school and still continued to take web development and, later, computer networking classes at the community college. I also enrolled in Eastern Michigan University on a whim and ended up getting an MBA in nonprofit management. Additionally, I got certified as an adult literacy tutor and then as a trainer for adult literacy tutors.

Of course, I pursued all these things because I was interested in them, but I also felt an intense compulsion to diversify the hell out of my skill set. I couldn't stand the thought of not feeling employable again after how long my library search had gone. On some level, I was also probably afraid that if I didn't keep adding to my résumé, I would end up thinking I needed to be a sex worker again to make ends meet if I lost my job, and I would be back on the getting fluctuating anxiety over the hustling roller coaster.

There is a much more visible dialogue within the library profession now about the lack of jobs available to new grads than there was when I graduated. I had felt like I was alone when I had so much trouble finding a job, but there were plenty of other people just like me. And from what I can tell, there are now even more unemployed or underemployed library school grads looking for professional work. It has become a joke in the library field about all the supposed new library jobs that were going to open up due to baby boomers retiring. For a while, "librarian" had been consistently listed in many different places as a job that would need new recruits in the future. That was why so many of us had gone to library school—we kept hearing the rhetoric that a bunch of jobs would be opening up. Instead, many of those jobs were either phased out when someone retired, or they were split into two part-time positions so the library could save money by not paying benefits.

As it currently stands, it is not uncommon to see public librarian job postings that are part-time and only pay fifteen dollars an hour. They can get away with that because the supply far outweighs the demand in terms of available librarians looking for jobs. There is no return on investment with these jobs, especially if you go to an out-of-state school and take out significant student loans, as I did. I often see the most diligent library school grads working on branding themselves with blogs and networking online. Many of them seem to maintain a much more positive attitude than I did when I was looking, so I salute them for preserving their enthusiasm.

More people are aware of how underpaid teachers are, but most librarians, at least those working in public libraries, are making a lot less, which seems unfair in a profession that demands a master's degree to be a part of. Besides librarians, I am unaware of any other types of professionals, outside of social workers, who get paid so little while still requiring so much formal education. It is difficult for librarians to organize to combat low wages, though, when so many of us are working in individual town and city libraries, where the guidelines for pay vary wildly. I once found out that someone in the same position as me, who worked just a town over, was making at least $15,000 more a year. That person also had a union, though, and we did not.

Sometimes a friend will want me to talk to one of their friends who is thinking about entering library school and looking for advice. I've never told anyone to turn away and not look back, but I've been pretty frank with people because I want them to know what they are getting into. At the end of the day, I still think it's a fulfilling and interesting career, and I'm still glad I did it. I just wish it hadn't been so hard to actually break into. I tell them to make sure they know that being a librarian is what they really want to do, make sure they get experience while they are still in grad school, and not roll their eyes at cheesy networking opportunities the way I used to. Also, they should know that they may be working multiple part-time jobs—for some people, this lasts for years—before they can find a steady full-time job in a public library.

22

This chapter was adapted from a presentation I did called "Building Revolutionary Solidarity Across the Profession" at the 2018 Urban Libraries Conference.

Fourteen years have passed since I've stripped. Since then, I've become something of a library vigilante, getting involved in a number of campaigns that helped combat the creep of private interests into public libraries. I've also spoken at conferences about how to effectively and collectively fight administrations that allow these things to happen through direct action, community organizing, and large-scale professional solidarity.

The first administration I learned to fight was my old one at Westland Public Library. Westland is a working-class city of eighty-five thousand people just a little outside of Detroit. I was the head of Technology Services and worked there for five and a half years, and my formal reason for resigning was to stay home with my son after he was born. I had been frustrated beyond hope, though, with the director and the appointed board and the irresponsible decisions they kept making about the library's policies and the way the staff was treated. As a department head, I would get stuck in three-hour department-head meetings where the director picked her victim of the week and decided we all had to talk about how terrible that person was. I started deciding to just exaggerate technology emergencies to get out of those toxic meetings. There was no maternity-leave policy, and the director changed the terms of the way we had agreed to use my FMLA weeks into the middle of my time home, after giving birth, simply because she could. I came back for two months so I could transition all of my programs, including the adult literacy program I started, as well as find someone to take over the library's technology needs. I gave two weeks' notice and left on good terms with everyone, quietly disappearing from library land. In the meantime, I went on to have another child and became the executive director at a small literacy nonprofit. I also published two books in a young adult dystopian thriller series called The Departed, where there was a conspiracy to fake the rapture. Frankly, I wasn't sure if I wanted to make the return to libraries after my experience at Westland.

About five years after I left Westland, I was scrolling Facebook one night and found a note written from the Westland teen librarian announcing how sad she was to be leaving the library. She and the majority of the librarians in the Reference department had been unexpectedly terminated, and all teen events had been canceled. She encouraged any teens who had questions about this decision to contact the director and gave everyone the date of the next board meeting.

I was furious. I had heard things had just gotten worse since I had left Westland and the administration had just escalated things big-time. I found out five librarians in the eight-person reference department I used to be in had been told they were "laid off." This made no sense to me because I had previously made all of the additional operational millage campaign literature myself. The millage that ensured their positions were budgeted for another five years and had passed by 70%. They had also turned in union intention papers just two days before the termination, which is something the board would go on to claim was just a coincidence.

I decided to go to the next board meeting, and one of the librarians asked me to livestream it so her parents could watch. I figured why not. This would clearly be a contentious meeting, and people should find out what was going on there. The meeting ended up being a three-ring circus. The board president tried to shout me down when he realized I was recording him. He claimed that they had to let people go to increase efficiencies, despite the fact that there were no clear money issues. A bunch of people ended up sharing the video, and in the end we had over seventeen thousand people watch it. We had a friend who shared it on one of the library school LISTSERVS, so I thought why not share it with the entire state library LISTSERV. I knew they were still trying to recruit part-time "library associates" to replace the librarians, so I felt like, at the very least, this was an easy way to let any potential applicant know what they were walking into.

As a result of my email to the state LISTSERV, one of the associates rescinded a job offer, and the board president sent an email response out to the LISTSERV, personally attacking me, discussing my personal HR information which wasn't even true, and attempting to justify their asinine rationale for the mass removal of librarians. As a result, he recruited a bunch of other librarians to support our cause and basically sucked me into this whole thing even more.

Since I had done the video with my personal Facebook account, my page became the de facto place to find out about what was happening at Westland, especially since the library had decided to take its own Facebook page down. I was also in the unique position to say whatever I wanted since I wasn't one of the people terminated and did not have to worry about how that might affect an unfair-labor-practice lawsuit.

We created a secret Facebook group for librarians who were supporting us that grew to three hundred members. They helped share a lot of my posts, and many of them emailed the mayor about how abnormal this kind of thing was. Along with Westland citizens, we showed up to city council en masse. Then there was a sudden closed library-board study session scheduled. The rumor coming out of the city was that the director was going to be fired. We knew that the mayor wanted this; however, we wanted the librarians to get their jobs back as well, which he had yet to say he supported. I scheduled a protest, we got a lot of labor rights organizations involved, and we even had three local news stations come out. However, the board dug in and insisted they were 100 percent behind the director and there was no way they were going to reverse their decision. I should note here that the board is completely appointed by the mayor. These are all people he picked. This was his board, and they were defying him.

So, essentially, we had to take down the director and the entire library board to restore proper library staffing and services at this library. In order to have them legally removed on the grounds of either misconduct or neglect of duty, the librarians would have had to prove it in a long, drawn-out court case. I'm not a very patient person, and I couldn't wait around for that. Luckily, the librarians gave me permission to go gangbusters.

Another big factor that stood in our way was that the local paper would only interview the board president about what had happened at the library, so we had to find a way to get the real story out to the Westland community. I began what I called a public information campaign in the form of a Facebook page I called Save the Westland Library. I raised money and boosted posts. I posted stats that showed how understaffed Westland was compared to other libraries.

I also found a creative way to enlist the help of some celebrities by going to Comic Con. I got a picture of LeVar Burton and Wil Wheaton holding We Love Westland Librarians signs. I posted it to the Facebook page with the caption "LeVar Burton of Reading Rainbow and Star Trek: TNG is judging you, Westland Library board. Way to piss off the guy who taught millions of kids to love reading by firing a bunch of librarians!" It got forty-five thousand views. For my Wil Wheaton one, I posted "When Star Trek actor, geek blogger, and librarian fan, Wil Wheaton, heard that the Westland Library board terminated a bunch of their librarians, his remarks were not very family friendly… 'Well f*** those guys then!'" It got twenty-five thousand views.

We went to the Westland inaugural State of the City address. One of our friends on city council gave us the in on where to sit to be most visible on the cameras, since we were all wearing bright-orange shirts that said "I Stand with Westland Librarians." At one point, we stood during his speech and sat back down. At the end, the mayor acknowledged us and said he stood with us too. He literally had to say he supported us or he would look like a jerk. The man was a democrat, but as I discovered getting more and more into political activism, that kind of distinction doesn't mean a whole lot, especially at the local level.

During all of this, we kept going back to city council and attending library board meetings. The attention the board was getting was affecting them. They began resigning one by one but not before making several other ridiculous moves in the process, including making the administrative assistant the assistant director. And when there were only three of them left, they voted to cut the millage in half from .99 mils to .50 mils, because the mayor told them they should no longer pursue their building expansion plans.

We had on open letter from me as well as six other former librarians, telling everyone that it was our consensus opinion that the director was unfit to lead this library and, by extension, the board was unfit because of their full support of her, despite all evidence of her poor leadership.

Did I mention it was an election year? Yeah, that helped us a lot! I sent out surveys about the library and the library's administration to everyone running for mayor and city council. There were sixteen people running for four seats, so it was a very contentious race. The mayor knew he had these survey results coming out soon that would not look very favorable for him if he didn't do anything. The other big thing that had happened was that the remains of the library board had fired the city attorney and hired their own independent council. The local paper wrote all about it since that reporter really liked interviewing the board president.

The other thing that helped put the final nail in the coffin was when I raised the question of why this board had been singularly interested in hundreds of thousands of dollars in building-improvement projects as well as this expansion that got tabled. They kept pointing out that they were volunteers, and I started asking why. Who volunteers to plan a bunch of building-improvement projects for an institution none of them used? Why did they never address policy, services, patron needs, or staff issues? Why didn't they know what the library actually did or anything about all of the programming that got canceled? I suggested that maybe I should start FOIA'ing all of their correspondences with every contractor involved with each project.

Suddenly, the mayor got the remaining board members to resign. Then the director resigned because she knew there was no one left to protect her, and he personally called all of the librarians to offer them their jobs back. I am confident the mayor would have never changed his tune had we not remained relentlessly obnoxious and incredibly organized. He wanted us to go away, and three months and ten days later, he finally accepted that we wouldn't.

I put my summary of what I learned through this experience on Facebook:

In the scheme of things, taking on an authoritarian library regime is small potatoes (after they engaged in the mass removal of librarians), but I learned a lot in terms of addressing authoritarianism in general:

- The system alone will not work, and even if it does, it will take five times longer than it should.

- Facts are never enough.

- Appeals to human decency won't work.

- You can't trust the press to accurately cover the story (even when you present them those same verifiable facts).

- Be very open to unconventional methods.

- You should look for allies anywhere and everywhere.

- Don't be afraid to make a spectacle.

- Clickbait the hell out of your message.

- Dig deep to uncover underlying motivations.

- Infographics!

- Remain relentlessly obnoxious and incredibly organized.

- The potential for humiliation and censure are highly motivating.

- Just because the main players are gone, doesn't mean it can't happen again. Sure, we can get better people leading the board and the library (or another regime), but at the end of the day, the same structures are in place that can allow this kind of thing to happen again. A democratically elected board would help, but it still wouldn't ensure accountability the way a less hierarchical governance structure (or even better, a nonhierarchical structure) would.

Ultimately, the librarians got their union vote of twenty-seven to five with SEIU 517M.

A few months later, I was connected with someone who worked at the Public Library of Cincinnati and Hamilton County after one of their board members publicly stated that they should sell a major downtown library building because it was a "prime piece of real estate." Also, their board was composed of a bunch of extremely affluent people with major ties in the local corporate and development community, and of course, they were all appointed. The current board president also happened to be on the board of the development consultancy, 3CDC, that the library hired to explore the option of consolidating their downtown building. Of course, they came back with the recommendation that it was in fact a good idea. The fact that this building served a significant homeless population and majority Black population likely contributed to their views on its disposability.

Once again, I went into library vigilante mode and drove down to Cincinnati to attend their next board meeting and meet with a growing group of local organizers who wanted to stop the sale of this building. I couldn't just say I was some librarian from Michigan who fucked shit up for a board in another community, so I created a Facebook page and started an organization called the Library Defense Network. I explained that our mission was to mobilize communities to fight for their library rights. I realized I knew exactly what to do to launch a public pressure campaign and was able to advise everyone on what they needed to do to get started. In my public comments at their packed library board meeting, I warned the board that this public outcry was not a one-off. These people would be back, and they would not stop. And I was right.

Initially, this library board did the opposite of the Westland board. While they weren't talking too much and putting their feet in their mouths, they ended up damning themselves with their silence. This board refused to engage with the public and didn't respond to any public comments at their meetings. We were able to get good local press in the *Cincinnati Enquirer* and *City Beat*.

We were also able to tell a compelling story when a patron got arrested for advocating for the library inside the library. He was wearing a sandwich board sign that said "3CDC: Hands off our Library!" and the security staff gave him a citation for criminal trespassing after he wouldn't turn his sign inside out. He was also banned from the library for six months. This story got a lot of press, and by the next day, the library rescinded his ban and apologized to him with reporters recording it for the local news. It probably helped that he was a white man with a PhD. I was able to take this story and get *Library Journal*, the biggest professional publication in the US, to cover it as well. In the story, the director claimed the building was being closed for financial reasons. She was not going to advocate for her patrons and library system but was just going to do what the library board told her to do.

This board was appointed, so there was no direct way to pressure them. In Ohio, all of the county systems have seven-member boards, where four of them are appointed by the county commissioners and three are appointed by the Court of Common Pleas. Since the court is a judiciary body with lifetime appointments, we had no leverage to use to pressure them, but we could pressure the commissioners, and that began to work. The county commissioners reached out to the board and asked for an explanation, but they ended up not being happy with the answers they got. They also weren't happy with the board's refusal to engage with the public on their plans for the North Building, so they formally requested the board have a public event about the building

The board scheduled a public "listening session," and the coalition did all of the work to actually publicize the event. The listening session was conducted by a $40,000 consultant, who facilitated the questions and told people they couldn't make any noise. The board didn't respond to any of the questions directly, and the consultant explained to everyone that they were just there to listen. A scathing article about how ridiculous this listening session was came out in the *Cincinnati Enquirer*, and the county commissioners told the board and the director that they had to do this again, but this time they had to actually talk. After it was very clear that public opinion was against the sale, the board finally called a special meeting to announce they weren't selling the building. This took four and a half months.

I realized I'd found my very specific niche and started advising library workers who didn't feel safe speaking out when their administrations made bad decisions that were detrimental to public services and the dedicated people who worked in libraries. I also got involved with several local organizing initiatives and began making some political connections. When my kids' school district was considering giving away a popular middle school to the more affluent county, I knew what to do. I had begun seeing how to make change through a much bigger lens than just voting and hoping elections would solve all of society's problems. I found that the most helpful allies on these campaigns were often not politicians, and the politicians you would expect to be supportive often weren't—or were only up for paying lip service.

Since I launched the Library Defense Network, I've had to slow down some of my organizing energy due to some health issues and adapting to being a single mom with two jobs. The Architect and I separated, and I moved out into an apartment. We arranged our own 50/50 custody schedule of our kids. I was already running a small cooperative house-cleaning company, but I needed to make more money to make it on my own, so I started applying for library jobs again.

I had launched myself into the whole library-vigilante thing without planning to go back into libraries. I had been burned by dedicating myself at Westland, and didn't expect to necessarily be employable in Michigan libraries again after the reputation I had built for myself as a troublemaker. At the same time, getting involved in libraries again at the advocacy level reminded me why I'd gone into them to begin with, and I felt a sense of rededication to the greater library objective. I also needed to better materially support myself, and libraries were the field I had the most training in.

I did find out some local library directors were afraid of me. However, none of those people actually knew me personally. There were others, though, that thought the work I did was important and appreciated the perspective I added. And of course, there were some directors who weren't really paying attention and had no idea who I was anyways. I was navigating a more complicated librarian job market than my first time around. I got lucky, though, and got a part-time adult-services position at a library where I already knew a few people. I was told it would all depend on my cover letter and interview, but I suspect it helped that they had seen me as a normal librarian before and not just the fighting person I could become in the right context.

I have now been there three years and am still part-time like most people at my library. There is not much room for advancement, and there are not a lot of other area libraries I can apply to, so I'm making it work with my cleaning business to supplement my income. I have no retirement, and I feel like I may always be chasing financial security, but we also live in a world where fewer and fewer people are achieving the kind of financial stability necessary to retire. At one point, there was the expectation that if you entered the so-called professional class, you could trust that your future basic needs would be met, but as with more and more professions, librarianship does not promise this. Some of the library schools may still be making this claim, but it isn't true for a good chunk of people who go into this work. A lot of the time, I feel like these part-time positions assume you're someone's wife (83 percent of librarians are women after all) and you don't need healthcare.

When I look back, I wish I had stayed in sex work longer, while I could still swing it. Not many people will admit regretting never becoming a full-service whore, but I will. I could have amassed the money I needed to make it more easily as a part-time librarian and single mom. Even more importantly, I could have had more time to dedicate myself to my library defense work and other political organizing. I'm good at fighting the powers that be, but like everyone else, I'm caught in the wage worker's bind, and there are very few jobs that pay you to be a fighter for a better world.

It's such an absurd idea that sex workers are the only ones selling themselves. All workers sell their time and labor. Sex workers just often get a better payout for their time.

Afterword

—◆○◆—

Sex work is an umbrella term for people who sell sex—or performances, materials, or services associated with sex acts—as their work.

What used to specifically constitute stripping vs. escorting vs. porn is becoming a grayer and grayer area. When I danced, I had met strippers who escorted and escorts who used to strip, but the lines are getting even fuzzier now. There are still clubs and geographic areas where what constitutes a lap dance is relatively enforced, but overall, the trend is toward blurrier and blurrier lines. And when I think about it, they were already getting fuzzy when I was in the clubs, judging by just how much more close contact was happening during dances than there had been even fifteen year before. Although I was supposed to be a stripper in the clubs, I still found a way to sometimes be a dominatrix who just didn't happen to have a dungeon nearby.

When the 2020 pandemic started and many strip clubs closed, a lot of strippers went online and began experimenting with other kinds of sex work, like camming and selling pictures. Some started Onlyfans accounts and began building brands, which could launch them into the next phases of their careers or also function as a way to keep customers engaged with them while not being able to see them in the clubs. Barely any in-person sex workers were promoting themselves online when I stripped, but now it's a lot more common. "Sex work" just covers it all and suggests a fluidity that varies from person to person.

The sex worker community online is a lot more robust than it was in the mid-aughts, which expands the possibility of greater solidarity. Sex worker Twitter and Instagram have rich interconnected communities that make it increasingly possible to share notes on clubs, management problems, and experiences with customers. Social media is also a place where sex workers can feel seen and understood because the civilians in our lives outside sex work may not quite understand our jokes as well as people who deal with the same kinds of customers do. In addition to being able to find more community online, there is a lot of sex-worker organizing going on. Some are organizing mutual aid funds, and others are educating people on decriminalization and getting SESTA/FOSTA overturned.

FOSTA (Fight Online Sex Trafficking Act) and SESTA (The Stop Enabling Sex Traffickers Act) are bills that became one law on April 11, 2018, in the United States. This bill essentially made platforms more liable for hosting content by third parties who may be "knowingly facilitating sex trafficking." The language of the bill is sufficiently vague, and a number of major websites that sex workers used to advertise on were shut down. The lawmakers who put these bills together thought they were going to help stop sex trafficking, but what happened was that they made sex work less safe for those doing their own advertising and actually increased the likelihood that someone might be susceptible to trafficking.

Criminalizing online information about sex work has wide legal implications for anyone even discussing sex work online. This includes not just advertising for sex work or soliciting sex work but also discussing how to do it and, even more importantly, how to do it safely. SESTA/FOSTA, however, didn't fully succeed at shutting down online advertising for sex work. Like many things on the Internet, people have found work-arounds. Sex workers who advertise online have found ways to do so through offshore websites, and customers have adapted to looking in different places to find their advertisements. In the process, the way to advertise has become more complicated and requires more technological savvy and a firm understanding of how of online privacy works. In the past, it was easier for sex workers to make quick and simple postings on websites like craigslist and Backpage (which is no longer available). If you want to advertise online now, though, you need to have a website, know what sites you can link your profiles to, communicate with customers, and be familiar with how to safely navigate social media.

Although some sex workers have found these work-arounds, there are still many who have not. Not only do they require a lot more upfront planning and work, but they also require a knowledge base that isn't accessible to many people, especially those who are new to sex work. If you can't advertise online, and sex work is your only option for income, then working on the street is the only alternative. Street sex work is significantly less safe. You don't have a trail of information about your customer that you can share with a trusted source ahead of time, and customers who seek sex workers on the street are aware of this (most online sex workers will require that a customer give references to other sex workers they've met, as a safety precaution). Additionally, you are more likely to be harassed or arrested by police posing as johns if you are working on the streets. You're also more susceptible to pimps who are offering protection but requiring a cut of your earnings and often giving you a quota as well. Online sex work gives sex workers significantly more autonomy, freedom, and safety options.

Sex-worker activists will tell you that it is a privilege to still be able to advertise online. Those I've spoken with told me they had more resources and access to mentors to help them set up their platforms. Like every other profession, those who have race, class, literacy, and cis privilege have an advantage. Not everyone has the resources to set up a website or knows someone who can help them. Many also don't have the luxury of time to plan all of these things in advance. Many sex workers do this kind of work on the side as needed, but there isn't a safe way for them to plug in easily when they need to find customers and work now.

SESTA/FOSTA also further restricts sex workers from helping each other online, which many of them have relied on to do this kind of work safely in the past. Providing information about how to do sex work safely, like using encrypted email and messaging apps, could be considered a form of trafficking as well. Sex workers can't connect with each other as easily through online mentorship because more sex workers are wary of offering that kind of information digitally to someone they don't know. There are small groups in some cities that do outreach to street sex workers about how to work safely online, but sex workers won't be able to find these organizations themselves. They have to be lucky enough to be found.

In addition to having to be careful online, many sex workers are subject to shadowbanning as a result of SESTA/FOSTA. is the act of blocking a user's content on social media sites, in such a way that the user doesn't know it's happening. If you're shadowbanned on Instagram for example, your content won't appear on anyone's feed unless they already follow you. Basically, the social media algorithms are tweaked to make sure you can't expand your reach, which can seriously conflict with connecting to new customers.

One of the groups working to help sex workers use more secure technology is Hacking Hustling, which is a collective of sex workers, survivors, and accomplices working at the intersection of tech and social justice to interrupt state surveillance and violence facilitated by technology. Their mission is to "abolish carceral technologies and build the capacity of sex workers and survivors to create new technologies that increase safety. [Their] work explodes the definition of technology to include harm reduction models: community-based research, mutual aid, organizing, art, and any/all tools sex workers and survivors develop to mitigate state, workplace, and interpersonal violence and thrive."

Here are their principles of unity (Inspired by INCITE! Women of Color Against Violence and Collective Action for Safe Spaces) and likely of interest to other organizer nerds:

We oppose the use of technology to enable state violence, including state surveillance cameras, law enforcement body cameras, sex offender registries, electronic monitoring, facial recognition technologies, and policing. We oppose all forms of oppression by state and non-state actors, recognizing the state as the central organizer of violence that oppresses people in the sex trades.

We understand technology to be more than the Internet and digital interfaces/devices.

We understand sex workers to be originators of new technologies and methods of keeping each other safe. These new technologies include early adoption of online platforms, sharing of online and physical bad date lists, safe calls, protest safety protocols, street art, art and cultural ephemera, and all harm reduction strategies.

We center the experiences, voices, and needs of people who trade sex by choice, circumstance, or coercion, and understand the overlap in these communities. We respect every person's autonomy in defining their own experiences.

We do not align ourselves with violence of the Non-Profit Industrial complex which has enabled a schism between people who trade sex by choice, circumstance or coercion for its own profit and political gains.

We build connections between liberation struggles opposing racism, sexism, classism, heterosexism, cissexism, ableism, capitalism, and all forms of oppression.

We promote shared leadership and collective decision-making. Using transparent structures for decision-making and conflict resolution, we work to be accountable to these principles not only in our public facing work but in our organizational practices.

We will not accept any federal or state funding for Hacking//Hustling activities.

Source: https://hackinghustling.org

What struck me when I read this list was how well sex-worker advocates frame the burgeoning surveillance state as a critical factor in understanding and protecting privacy. It may seem more obvious why sex workers and their customers need to protect their privacy than it would seem for other people, but the issue of privacy is something that is only going to continue to grow as the data economy expands. Although the average civilian may not have to worry about their data getting leaked and having people find out you do sex work, big data breaches affect hundreds of millions of people's personal records every year.

Data is now more valuable than oil, and it is the biggest commodity being traded through Google, Amazon, Facebook, Microsoft, and Apple. Our apps keep track of our browsing history, use GPS to track our habits, and listen in to our conversations to deliver us custom-tailored advertising. Our use becomes what can be sold to us, and this is something people are beginning to call surveillance capitalism. Another technology that looms on the privacy-nightmare horizon is facial-recognition technology. Unlike apps, we give no consent when it's being used. It's not regulated, and there are many documented false positives, as well as racial bias. Furthermore, it's a big threat to free speech and protest. This kind of technology is still so new that we've yet to really learn what the long-term consequences of giving up our privacy to corporations and the state will be. For this reason, the privacy advocacy of sex workers benefits everyone.

Librarians traditionally have been an authority on upholding privacy rights, but sex workers are taking their place. Confidentiality and privacy are library core values; patrons can trust that they can check out whatever they want without us divulging that information to a third party. Librarians also help patrons with better privacy practices when they come into the library to set up online accounts, like making a strong password and storing it safely. We also pushed back hard on the Patriot Act's Section 215, which said that librarians had to hand over patron reading and computer records when those items were requested by law enforcement. We believe in intellectual freedom and the right to research. Those rights can be preserved only if patron privacy is respected. In more recent times, though, libraries have unfortunately shifted away from our historical hardline privacy stance because we've been too influenced by the dominant, data-driven culture. I think this is in part, too, because we're so afraid of having our budgets and services cut and think that we need to keep up with corporate platforms and collect tons of data in the same way they do in order to stay relevant.

For this reason, I saw a synthesis of common interests that hasn't really been pursued by anyone yet. I explored this overlap when I participated in the Library Freedom Institute's second cohort. Library Freedom Institute (LFI) is a privacy-focused four-month program for librarians to teach the skills necessary to thrive as privacy advocates, from educating community members to influencing public policy. We explore all of the different kinds of threats to privacy—government and police surveillance, big data, malware, fraud, identity theft. There is so much room to expand libraries into further protective spaces for patrons.

All participants in LFI do group projects. My group did our project on educating other library workers about SESTA/FOSTA, and I interviewed a few current sex-worker activists on their privacy practices. I learned that librarians have a lot to learn from sex workers about privacy advocacy. Some other group projects include tools that teach people about facial-recognition technology, library-vendor privacy scorecards, privacy-policy templates, and guides to defending your data. LFI has had four cohorts now and is working on achieving the professional reach necessary to get librarianship back to prioritizing privacy. You can learn more about LFI at https://libraryfreedom.org

The library model of data privacy is clearly superior to the corporate model. While much of our data may be under the control of a small handful of private companies, accountable to none but their shareholders, libraries are accountable to their communities. I really think that library values and practices, like equitable access and efficiently allocating shared resources, have a lot to offer to conversations about how we organize our world.

Please check out the Additional Resources section if you're interested in learning more about sex work, decriminalization, and privacy advocacy, as well as some kick-ass sex-worker accounts to follow on social media.

If you enjoyed this book, please consider leaving a review on Amazon and/or Goodreads.

You can also learn about my future projects by signing up for my newsletter, and learn more about my other books by visiting kristycooper.com.

Additional Resources

I don't consider these lists to be exhaustive. There are definitely other valuable books, websites, and social media accounts to follow, but these are some good ones to help get you started.

BOOKS

Coming Out Like a Porn Star: Essays on Pornography, Protection, and Privacy edited by Jiz Lee

I've Got to Make My Livin': Black Women's Sex Work in Turn-of-the-Century Chicago by Cynthia M. Blair

Playing the Whore by Melissa Gira Grant

Revolting Prostitutes by Juno Mac and Molly Smith

Sex, Lies & Statistics by Dr. Brooke Magnanti

Sex Work Matters by Melissa Hope Ditmore

Sex Workers, Psychics, and Numbers Runners: Black Women in New York City's Underground Economy by LaShawn Harris

Strange Times: Tales From American Strippers by Elle Stanger

Striptastic by Jacqueline France

Thriving in Sex Work: Heartfelt Advice for Staying Sane in the Sex Industry: A Self-Help Book for Sex Workers by Lola Davina

To Live Freely in This World by Chi Adanna Mgbako

WEBSITES

Black Sex Worker Collective

    https://www.blacksexworkercollective.org

Decoding Stigma

    https://decodingstigma.tech

Hacking Hustling

    https://hackinghustling.org

Library Freedom Project

    https://libraryfreedom.org

Lysistrata: A Mutual Care Collective & Fund

    https://www.lysistratamccf.org

Sex Workers Outreach Project - SWOP-USA

    https://swopusa.org

SWARM (Sex Worker Advocacy and Resistance Movement)

    https://www.swarmcollective.org

SOCIAL MEDIA

Twitter

@BodyByBlunts

@HeauxHistory

@Lola_Davina

@LysistrataMCCF

@MissLoreleiLee

@MsMaggieMayhem

@prolepeach

@RebelleCunt

@RedCanarySong

@SinnamonLove

@swopbehindbars

@swopusa

@thatgirlfierce

@TheBlackSWC

Instagram

The BSWC
    @thebswc
Elle Stanger, CSE
    @stripperwriter
Gizelle Marie
    @thegizellemarie

Jacq Frances

    @jacqthestripper

LysistrataMutualCareCollective

    @lysistratamccf

MF AKYNOS

    @akynos

Selena The Stripper

    @prettyboygirl

Sex Work History

    @sexworkhistory

Sex Workers Project @ UJC

    @sexworkersproject

Strippers United

    @soldiers_of_pole_

About the Author

Kristy Cooper is a librarian single mom in Michigan. In her spare time, she fights politicians for libraries and will eventually get around to finishing writing her YA series.

Website: kristycooper.com
Facebook: facebook.com/librarydefense
Twitter: twitter.com/librarydefend
Instagram: instagram.com/stripper.librarian

Acknowledgements

Several people were vital in helping me write and complete this book. I want to thank my beta readers Sarah Rigg, Cassandra Mackie, Anne Cnockaert, and Cassie Schissell Barber for all of their fantastic feedback. I'm also incredibly grateful for my editors Sarah Carleton of Red Adept Editing and Luna Hughson. I sat on the first draft of this manuscript for a long time, and these people were critical in helping me bring it back to life.

Finally, I want to thank the countless people I've told about this book that assured me the world was ready for it and they would support me when I came out as a former sex worker. I'm also indebted to the inspiration of the many other sex workers I've seen come out and share their stories.